AUTISM MOTHERS
SPEAK OUT

of related interest

Maria and Me
A father, a daughter (and Autism)
Maria Gallardo and Miguel Gallardo
ISBN 978 1 78592 381 4
eISBN 978 1 78450 729 9

A Parents' ABC of the Autism Spectrum
Stephen Heydt
ISBN 978 1 78592 164 3
eISBN 978 1 78450 435 9

Sometimes Noise is Big
Life with Autism
Angela Coelho
Illustrated by Camille Robertson
ISBN 978 1 78592 373 9
eISBN 978 1 78450 719 0

A Guide to Sometimes Noise is Big for Parents and Educators
Angela Coelho and Lori Seeley
Illustrated by Camille Robertson
ISBN 978 1 78592 374 6
eISBN 978 1 78450 720 6

AUTISM MOTHERS SPEAK OUT

STORIES OF ADVOCACY AND ACTIVISM FROM AROUND THE WORLD

Edited by
Maggi Golding and Jill Stacey

Jessica Kingsley *Publishers*
London and Philadelphia

First published in 2018
by Jessica Kingsley Publishers
73 Collier Street
London N1 9BE, UK
and
400 Market Street, Suite 400
Philadelphia, PA 19106, USA

www.jkp.com

Library of Congress Cataloging in Publication Data
Names: Golding, Maggi, editor. | Stacey, Jill, editor.
Title: Autism mothers speak out : stories of advocacy and activism from around the world / edited by Maggi Golding and Jill Stacey.
Description: London ; Philadelphia : Jessica Kingsley Publishers, 2018.
Identifiers: LCCN 2017058452 | ISBN 9781785925153 (alk. paper)
Subjects: LCSH: Mothers of autistic children. | Autistic children. | Autism in children.
Classification: LCC HQ773.8 .A98 2018 | DDC 305.9/084083--dc23 LC record available at https://lccn.loc.gov/2017058452

British Library Cataloguing in Publication Data
A CIP catalogue record for this book is available from the British Library

ISBN 978 1 78592 515 3
eISBN 978 1 78450 906 4

Printed and bound in Great Britain

To all mothers of people with autism:
past, present and future.

CONTENTS

———————

INTRODUCTION

The term 'refrigerator mothers' came into common usage from the 1950s but reflected the views of psychoanalysts from the 1940s who focused on the mother's psychopathology. The perception was that mothers of autistic children lacked warmth and were unable to mother their children. It was thus believed that they caused their children's autism, and, because of this theory, it was likely that research and the understanding of autism was delayed for at least two decades.

When I met my first child with autism in 1957 I had no idea why this 4-year-old boy was always so distressed. He screamed if people came near him or tried to comfort him. He had no language and did not play or interact with the other children. Paul was one of 36 small children with developmental and learning difficulties who had been transferred from orphanages and institutions after the Second World War to a small residential school, to see if this would be an enabling environment. And so it was for 11 of the 12 children in the class group, but not for Paul. Older members of staff were convinced he needed to be 'disciplined', but none of the then-suggested approaches worked, and his plight occupied my mind even when I was off duty one and a half days each week.

Two years later, I was appointed to a teaching post at a new psychiatric children's hospital in High Wick, Hertfordshire, UK. Here, I found many children like Paul who were exhibiting strange behaviours. Some of them attacked those around them or hurt themselves. Most of the patients, as they were called, had no speech, and they did not interact socially. Paul was transferred to High Wick and I was surprised to see that his distress lessened and he started to make progress in my classroom in an environment where there were other children like him.

High Wick was run according to Freudian psychoanalytical principles,[1] and many famous experts such as Anna Freud, Dr Donald Winnicott and others were involved in training and support at the hospital. Initially, the children were labelled as psychotic or schizophrenic, but were later described as being severely emotionally disturbed and/or suffering from early childhood autism. This was seen as being a condition of early childhood which could be cured by psychoanalytical treatment for the mother to help her to be able to 'mother' and bond with her child. The child would be treated in play therapy where Freudian interpretations were made related to the child's behaviour. The implication was always that the autistic child had withdrawn from the real world and could be helped to overcome his autism. No one thought that children with autism would grow up into adults with autism.

In common with other experts in the field at High Wick hospital, the children's problem behaviours were believed to be due

---

1 Freud, S. (1973) *2: New Introductory Lectures on Psychoanalysis.* Harmondsworth: Pelican; Rycroft, C. (1972) *A Critical Dictionary of Psychoanalysis.* London: Penguin

to the family psychopathology and especially to the alleged lack of warmth or parenting abilities of the mothers.

Dr Leo Kanner, an Austrian American psychiatrist best known for describing 'early infantile autism'[2] in 1943, related the condition to what he described as a lack of warmth in the parents. In 1960, in an interview with *Time* magazine, he said that the parents just happened to 'defrost enough to produce a child'![3]

By now the term 'refrigerator mothers' had entered into common parlance.

Charismatic concentration camp survivor, Bruno Bettelheim, broadcast this belief across an array of television shows as well as other media. Bettelheim continually described autistic children as products of mothers who were distant, cold and rejecting, depriving their children of the chance to truly bond.

By this time, there was widespread acceptance of this belief by the medical profession and the general public.

In *The Empty Fortress*, Bettelheim compared children with autism to the plight of prisoners in a concentration camp.[4] Autism was now viewed as a disorder of parenting.

From 1940 through to the 1970s, Bettelheim was the Director of the University of Chicago's Orthogenic School and he stated that the children would benefit from a 'parentectomy'. The psychoanalytical world supported and further articulated this theory. For example, in his book *Interpretation of Schizophrenia* (1955), well-respected psychiatrist Sylvano Arieti[5] wrote about the mother–child relationship and how an autistic tendency is the sign of a disorder

---

2   Kanner, L. (1943) 'Autistic disturbances of affective contact.' *Nervous Child* 2, 217–250

3   Kanner, L. (1960) 'The child is father.' *Time* (25 July)

4   Bettelheim, B. (1967) *The Empty Fortress*. New York, NY: The Free Press

5   Arieti, S. (1955) *Interpretation of Schizophrenia*. New York, NY: Robert Brunner

in socialisation. He assumed that this implied a difficulty between a child and his parents.

Frances Tustin spent her professional life upholding this theory. She was adamant that one should note that autism is one of a number of children's neurological disorders of a psychogenic nature, and that it is caused by the abusive and traumatic treatment of infants. She referred to millions of children who were damaged because of cruel treatment by parents who were too busy to love and care for their babies.[6]

However, by the late 1960s, psychoanalytical theory began to lose its credibility due to several factors.

Bernard Rimland, a research psychologist and parent of a child with autism, was the first person to challenge the psychiatric orthodoxy about the cause of autism. In his 1964 book, *Infantile Autism: The Syndrome and Its Implications for a Neural Theory of Behaviour*, he questioned the theory of the unloving parent–child relationship and presented a fairly strong argument that autism was a biological and not a psychogenic condition.[7]

In the same year, Eric Schopler, in his doctoral research on the sensory preferences of children with autism, helped to redefine the condition as a developmental disability rather than a psychogenetic one caused by poor parenting.

In 1971, he described how parents were co-therapists and were primary developmental agents for their children. In writing about the project, he explained that the research showed that the parents reacted to the developmental disability rather than caused it.[8]

Many professionals in the field were puzzled that these

6   Tustin, F. (1991) 'Revised understanding of psychogenetic autism.' *International Journal of Psycho-Analysis 72*, 4, 585–591

7   Rimland, B. (1964) *Infantile Autism: The Syndrome and Its Implications for a Neural Theory of Behaviour.* London: Jessica Kingsley Publishers

8   Lewis, M. and Tapp, A. (2015) *Biography of Eric Schopler.* Narrative documents book 2. Available at: https://scholarexchange.furman.edu/schopler-about/2

so-called 'refrigerator mothers' had produced non-autistic siblings. At High Wick hospital, in informal talks with mothers, it seemed as though their psychoanalytical treatment was increasing their feelings of guilt about what they might have done wrong to be such 'bad' parents to their children with autism. In conversations when they came to collect their children from the schoolroom, most of them said that they accepted the theory that they were to blame and several of them said they were appreciative of the opportunity to have the treatment on offer so that they could undo the damage they had done. My main impression after listening to the mothers was that they were unhappy and often distressed, and I wondered what they had done with this particular child to make him/her autistic when they had other perfectly normal sons and daughters. Their commitment to the time and energy given to their treatment was outstanding. It spoke of their devotion to the child with autism. I was confused!

Then, after Bettelheim died in 1990, it was revealed by Richard Pollak, the brother of a person with autism, in his book, *The Creation of Dr B,* that his life story had been misconstrued.[9] Dr Bettelheim had, in fact, invented his credentials and expertise on autism and had popularised the 'refrigerator mother' theory without adequate proof.

However, for many years after there was anger and mistrust on the part of parents towards professionals and this extended towards all professionals, not just those in the medical field. At an inaugural meeting of parents who eventually founded the National Autistic Society in the UK, I was asked why I was attending as I was not a parent. When I described my work as an educator with children with autism, I was asked to entertain their children in the next room while the meeting took place!

Eventually, the theory was officially abandoned mainly because

9   Pollak, R. (1997) *The Creation of Dr B.* New York: Simon & Schuster

of political pressure from parents who, with Bernard Rimland, founded the Autism Society of America and gradually the parents of children with autism found a voice.

In 1962, in the UK and at the request of the government, the first school for children with autism, Edith Edwards House, was opened as a pilot venture by The Invalid Children's Aid Association (now known as I CAN). Psychogenic theories were not supported, and parents were encouraged to be part of their child's planning and education. It had become clear to educators that mothers were the victims of the autism, not the cause.

In the UK, the National Autistic Society began to set up its own schools, moving right away from psychoanalytic approaches and promoting autism-specific education.

Now the theory is officially widely discarded in the UK, the USA and where we, the authors, reside – South Africa. But, the theory has not completely gone away and, globally, mothers of children with autism do not always get a 'good press'.

In France and several other European countries, the theory still exists.

In South Korea in 2011, an international research team found that 2 per cent of the primary school population (ages 7 to 12 years) met the criteria for the diagnosis of autism – one in 38 children.[10] The 'refrigerator mother' is largely believed to be the cause of autism.

As recently as 2012 in Ireland, Tony Humphreys of the University of Cork supported the idea of 'frigid parenting' being the cause of autism. In an article in the *Irish Examiner* on 3 February 2012 he suggested a link between autism and parents not expressing love

---

10   Kim, Y.S., Koh, Y.J., Levethal, B.L. *et al.* (2011) 'Prevalance of autism spectrum disorders in a total population sample.' *American Journal of Psychiatry*, 168, 904–912

and affection to their young children.[11] He later defended his views on Irish national radio.

Although it is not necessarily overt, one still comes across professionals who perceive parents of learners with autism in a different way from parents of other disabled children. In a recent conversation I had with a young and warmhearted psychologist it became clear that somehow manifestations of autism itself and the parents' situations were not always understood. For example, the term 'those parents' was used when referring to parents of a child with autism where no names were given, yet only a few minutes before he had spoken positively about Jane and Tony, parents of a Down syndrome boy. When challenged, his defence was, 'but, you must admit those parents [pointing to the autism unit] are really difficult'. Perhaps a weekend spent with a family of a child with autism might modify this view!

Parents of children with autism are in a somewhat different situation from most parents of disabled children. As described in this book, the mothers give birth to a baby who appears to be quite normal and they have no reason to suspect their child is 'different'. Children with autism do not look any different from other children. In fact, they are often physically very attractive. There are no medical markers and it is only when atypical behaviours appear or difficulties in early communication and social development begin to be apparent that mothers are faced with a realisation that their child is very different from many other children. Thus begins the long process of diagnosis and, if they are lucky, placement in an autism-specific educational environment. Unfortunately, this first road is not always smooth, nor does it necessarily have the desired outcome even in the most affluent Western countries.

---

11   Humphreys, A. (2012) 'Core connection: A diagnosis of Asperger's syndrome does little to help a child troubled by unhappy relationships.' *Irish Examiner.* p.7

In discussions with many mothers from different cultures over a period of 40 years, I observed that receiving a diagnosis of autism affected them in many different ways but one of the first thoughts many expressed was, 'What did I do or not do that might have caused my baby to develop into this child with social and communication difficulties, who is so different from other children and who cannot grasp the social rules governing everyday life?' It was not uncommon to hear that their own families blamed the mother for 'not disciplining' the child, or that it was said, 'We don't have this on our side of the family.' Mothers from some cultures were stigmatised as having 'bad blood' and it was not uncommon in some South African cultures to hear that the family was thought to be cursed and was treated accordingly.

All mothers talked about the shock of getting the diagnosis, having thought initially that they had given birth to a beautiful, normal baby. Even though by the time of the diagnosis they had begun to realise that their child probably was on the autism spectrum, one mother said it was as if someone had punched her in the stomach. Several of the mothers in different parts of the world expressed how traumatic it was to lose the child they originally thought they had. But inevitably, the mothers said how much this little person needed all the love they could give and that one had simply to carry on.

And carry on is what all the mothers who contributed to this book did, not only to benefit their own child but also to selflessly pave the way for others!

In deciding to put this book together we wanted to put 'refrigerator mothers' in the bin permanently – not to be recycled!

The stories come from a variety of countries and the grown-up children are from different parts of the autism spectrum. In some cases, the language used may seem a little outdated but we have kept it as it is to reflect the time and culture which the contributors are talking about.

The mothers' stories of their journeys are truly a celebration of love, commitment and heroism.

Enjoy!

Maggi Golding

Chapter 1

CAROLE AND JASON

(ENGLAND)

In 1971, after nine years of marriage, I became pregnant with my son, Jason. The pregnancy was normal until a month before when I had to go into hospital for bedrest. He was born two weeks later and thus two weeks early, on 26 April 1972, by a forceps delivery.

For the first eight months of his life, he was a happy, perfect baby, eating and sleeping contentedly. Then he got rubella. As he started growing up, we noticed he was different and he found it difficult to mix with other children, preferring to be alone. He started nursery school when he was 3 years old, but more and more problems emerged. Jason could not mix with other children and became disruptive if they would not let him join in with them and would spoil their games. His speech was delayed but he was potty trained very quickly before he started nursery. The nursery school recommended speech therapy and, by the time he left nursery

to start school in 1977, his speech was no longer a problem, but his co-ordination was not good, so he attended Guy's Hospital for exercises, which we also did at home. At this time, he saw a top doctor at Guy's Hospital who told us 'not to worry as he was a late developer and it would all come right in the end'. Jason stayed at primary school until July 1980 but we spent much of our time being called in to the school because of his behaviour and because he couldn't cope with the work. We feel he should have been diagnosed earlier and attended a special school, not a primary school, and it was three wasted years of his life.

Jason attended the junior school from September 1979 to July 1980 and the problems got worse. The headteacher, and we also agreed, felt he needed to move to a special school. Mention was made about finding him a suitable placement and the word 'autistic' was said. We had never heard of this term and we visited the library to find out what it was. After reading about the problems this handicap can cause, we felt he needed a specialist school. We visited a special school which had an autistic unit in it and, although we felt he was more able than some of the six other children in the unit, we were impressed with the teacher and support staff. This proved to be a good move, as his education came on leaps and bounds with the good teaching he received and in a small unit. Our son asked why he had to leave his school to go to another one. We explained to him that he was autistic, and it was a handicap and we had found him a special teacher in a small class of six children and this would help him.

In the summer holidays that year, I took him to a fete locally and while we were watching a display of mounted policemen he got bored and asked me if he could watch horse riding nearby. As it was near me, I agreed. When he came back he said to me, 'I have just had a ride on a horse.' I said to him, 'You have no money.' He told me that he said, 'Let's have a go', and when they asked for the money he replied, 'I am handicapped.' They asked what the handicap was and he said, 'My head is not working properly.' They told him to get on, so he got a free ride.

At the age of 11 years, in 1984, Jason had to leave his unit and the school tried to put him into other classes but, unfortunately, it didn't work out. We started looking around and found a weekly boarding school for autistic children. We joined their waiting list for a year, and he started there in January 1984 and left in July 1991. During this time, we  noticed he started doing strange things, such as undressing himself and dressing himself again and going back and touching things in the street. It was very difficult when out to get him to stop these rituals, which we now know are due to obsessive compulsive disorder (OCD). He also became very anxious on buses and was very difficult when the doors closed. When I was driving my car, he started trying to open the car door, so I used taxis a lot. His sleeping pattern was bad, and we were worn out when he kept coming into our bedroom, trying to get into our bed.

We were referred to the Maudsley Hospital Children's Department in South London when he was 9 years old and we requested a brain scan, which showed up nothing to help us with a diagnosis. We then attended the Maudsley Hospital every week as a family and he saw a doctor while we saw a social worker who tried to help us to cope each week. After a time, the appointments got less frequent and when he started the weekly boarding school they had a psychiatric social worker who visited us at home and saw him at school, which helped us enormously. In a drama lesson at the weekly boarding school they were acting out 'going to the moon' but Jason wouldn't accept it and stated that he could not leave his Mum to go to the moon, so he could not go. In his mind, it was real.

At that time, we lived in a flat and some new neighbours had moved in next door. When Jason came home on Friday evening he asked me if the new neighbours had moved in. I told him they had and because the man next door had had a nose operation, I explained this to our son, thinking if he saw the neighbour he would not ask what he had done. As we got into the lift the new neighbour was already in it and Jason straightaway said, 'Oh, are you our new neighbour with the thing on your nose?' I was so embarrassed.

The headteacher at his weekly boarding school suggested we look around at where he could go after leaving them in 1991. We visited some placements for young autistic adults, but we thought he was too bright to go to them. Some past pupils from his weekly boarding school had gone to a college in Grimsby where young adults learned how to cook, live independently and get experience of different trades in workshops. The college also found them employment after their courses ended and they returned home. Parents were expected to travel with them when they first started, collecting them and returning them to the college, but after a while they were taught to travel home alone. The weekly boarding school had started encouraging Jason to travel alone after initially travelling with him and then gradually letting him travel by himself (someone would sit in a different part of the public transport, then, when he was ready, they let him do it alone). Jason was able to travel home on his own at weekends by the time he left the weekly boarding school, so it helped him tremendously. He was always interested in routes and would spend hours drawing different road maps – once he had visited a place he could tell you exactly how to get home and was a good 'navigator'. After one outing, we came home via London Bridge Station and Jason looked at the South East Railway network on a board at the station. That night at home he drew the entire network, including all the little stations, after only once looking at the board – he has a fantastic memory for things like this.

We visited the college in Grimsby with Jason and were very impressed. We asked to go on the waiting list and were told it was a two-year course and we had to find the funding. We approached our local council for funding, but they agreed to fund him but only for one year because they stated they only had to fund his schooling until the age of 19 and he would be older if they funded two years. I read the Education Act and found out that in special cases, including autism, funding could be for longer. And so the battle began! We got a copy of the *Charities Digest* and we wrote to all the charities we thought would help us (over 80 letters), but no luck. We wrote to the Rowntree Trust – no reply. We were thinking of going on Esther Rantzen's show to say what an awful council we had.

We were then told about a specialist solicitor who acted in cases such as ours. Jason and I visited her and she took on the case. She found out that when Jason left his schooling the council should have sent us a statement of his special educational needs, which they had not done. The council then agreed to fund the two years and he started the college in August 1991, staying until July 1993. He started driving lessons while at Grimsby and when he returned to live at home again we found him a special needs driving instructor and he passed his test in 1996.

At the end of his course in July 1993, the work situation for young people was very difficult and there were no jobs so, where the college had before been able to settle their students into work after they left, it was no longer possible. Jason came back home to live and in September 1993 he enrolled at Lewisham College doing maths and English for a term and then, when the course ended, carried on with maths, English and computer work at Southwark College until February 1998. We had heard about a job agency in our area helping young adults with special needs to find employment, supported by a worker. Jason applied to join the agency and in May 1998 he started at NatWest Bank in London, working in the post room sorting out the post, with support from the job agency. However, the job agency had no experience of autism; Jason found the job boring and his colleagues did not understand him. He was very unhappy there, so he left in March 2002.

We then insisted he went back to college, so he joined Lambeth College to do four years on a computer course supported by a special educational needs co-ordinator, enabling him to get his certificates to find work in computers, which he loves. At that time, the National Autistic Society set up its own job agency with support workers. He joined up with them, went to their offices, and they practised interviewing for jobs and found him a job in the Civil Service, where he still works after 11 years. He applied for promotion to a higher grade in 2014 and was sent for an interview. In September 2015, he heard he had got the job and training started for four weeks in December 2015. He has been in post since then, finding the job very interesting. In 2015, the Civil Service allowed a course on autism awareness to be run by the National Autistic Society, helping staff to understand the problems of being autistic. Jason has found this very helpful, as staff now understand his problems.

His treatment at the Maudsley Hospital Children's Department covered the ages 8 to 17 years. Jason then attended the Mental Health Maudsley Hospital regarding his medication but, unfortunately, this was withdrawn in 2013 when his GP (doctor) was given the job of dealing with his tablets. We find this difficult because GPs are so busy now, the appointments are very short and many GPs have no experience of mental health or autism.

He still lives at home, as unfortunately he cannot afford to live independently. We obviously worry about him being 'independent' from us, as other young adults are, but there is no accommodation and we cannot afford to pay for it. Another worry is that he finds it difficult to make friends to socialise with, which is part of his autism. He has joined a chess club and was a member of a cycling club but dropped out after his bike had problems. He has since bought another bike but has not rejoined the club.

Jason has a friend in Lancaster, whom he met when he was at Grimsby College. He visits him about four times a year, and his friend lives independently now, since his parents bought him a house (properties are much cheaper there). His friend has been down to stay with us but with the cost of rail fares and his outgoings, it is easier for Jason to visit Lancaster, which has much more going for young people as it is a lively university town.

He still has OCD, which can be very bad when he is stressed out. He has many phobias, which are attached to the solar system and the weather (for example, rainbows and the full moon) and unfortunately he believes the superstitions he reads in books and on the computer, although we are trying to get him to stop doing this. At the moment, Jason is seeing, privately, a psychotherapist who also uses hypnotism to privde some relief for him.

We would recommend any people with autistic young children, teenagers or older younger adults to join the National Autistic Society. We have found the orgaisation so helpful when looking for schools and jobs, and for any other problems we have experienced.

Chapter 2

EDITH AND JUAN JOSÉ

(COLOMBIA)

Juan José is the youngest of three siblings. He developed typically until the age of 18 months, when he began to change his behaviours; he lost the little words he had acquired and began to show different attitudes in comparison to his brother and sister when they were the same age. After two years of seeking answers from several professionals, we were told that Juan José had autism. We found this strange, as he never expressed rejection to us and had always allowed us to pet, kiss and hug him.

The first reaction we had was sadness and uncertainty; my husband and I felt alone, the professionals we visited knew little about autism and we did not understand what was happening to our child. We talked to many health professionals and got few responses, so we started to look for a specialised institution for children with autism. We thought that would be the best choice for him, but eventually I noticed Juan José engaging in some behaviours of self-stimulation that I had seen in other children at the institution and so we decided to withdraw him. We set up a home programme for me to manage, with goals that we would evaluate periodically.

However, it was obvious that Juan José was growing up, and after a long search for kindergartens for him where we encountered deceptions and many rejections, eventually he was accepted at Rafael Pombo Garden.

For me and my family, the day Juan José received his preschool diploma was a huge achievement and we felt great pride and joy.

As Juan José grew older, we became conscious that an awareness campaign was needed for teachers and peers. After kindergarten, he was enrolled in a regular school – a school that gave him respect from his friends, other children and teachers. He really enjoyed his time at school, like any child, but the education process meant he required support in the classroom. We personally employed a facilitator (in Colombia we have no public policies that cover people with autism) and the school offered a flexible curriculum.

One of the most beautiful experiences I had with Juan José was when he was invited to the 'sweet 15' birthday of one of his friends! He had to go without family and in a tuxedo suit! It was a whole new experience for him, and for us! He chose the suit himself, the colour and everything. Our surprise was even greater when we found out that he was one of 15 young boys chosen to dance the waltz with the birthday girl! He only enjoyed the party until 11pm because he fell asleep! I am convinced that the respect, recognition and acceptance that Juan José had at school was a result of them acknowledging him as a person with abilities – loyal and a fighter – beyond his autism.

Juan José communicates through a program on an iPod that reproduces what he writes because he has no verbal language.

We achieved this due to the work of a professional team, where the phonoaudiologist directed his communication process. Juan José has received professional support since he was 2 years old, which has been adjusted according to his age.

As I write this chapter, Juan José is about to turn 19 years old. Last year he finished high school; he swims, rides a bike, skateboards, and is the happiest boy. He will have to begin a new stage and we, as a family too, will have to start again and try to open spaces to keep him learning and preparing for adult life and the community.

After telling you a little about my son, now I want to share a little about my life. I am Betty Roncancio Morales. I live in Bogotá, Colombia, and I am happily married. I have three children: Camila Andrea, 23 years old, Hector Daniel, 22 years old and Juan José, 18 years old.

When I found out that Juan José had autism, it was very hard for me. Not knowing or understanding what autism was, and its cause, made me and my husband feel very sad, desperate and alone. Also, we knew that the lack of knowledge of professionals and the community about this condition would accompany my son throughout his life.

When I speak or write about what Juan José has meant in my life, I cannot help but get emotional. He came into my life and definitely changed me as a person. He has taught me patience and love in another dimension and in an unconditional way. He teaches me that if everyone in the world had autism, the world would be a better place – there would be no lies, everyone would be punctual and, most of all, people would not need words to express love and tenderness. Juan José has changed my life so much that today I direct an organisation that works hard to promote the rights of people with autism in Colombia.

Juan José has made us one united family, with him at the

centre. His parents and his siblings love him unconditionally. We had a child who behaved, related and communicated differently. From the very beginning we thought that he had skills and that if we supported him and gave him the necessary tools, he would accomplish great things in life.

Autism impacts us 24 hours a day, 365 days a year. This makes families focus on exploring options to improve their difficulties, to learn how to interact and understand their child. In my case, I am fortunate to have a business with my husband, which has allowed us to give Juan José professional support from a young age through an interdisciplinary team, but we realise that our country should do more to change the situation of people with autism and their families.

And that is how Juan José has become my engine, which has prompted me to change my job. First, I was an accountant in our company and now I lead an organisation whose main objective has been to impact on public policies, raise awareness of people with autism as subjects with rights and duties, and seek alliances and teamwork with other mothers from different places of Colombia, all like me, motivated by the immense love they feel for their children.

Many people tell me that they admire us as a family for everything we do for our son, but what we do for Juan José is what any parent does for their child, whether they have autism or not. It is just that much more vital if the child has a disadvantage that makes it difficult to reach a world not designed for people like Juan José, where people know little about autism, believe in myths and paradigms and hardly understand what it means to be a parent of a child with autism. Despite the tears, sadness, and uncertainty, these children give you vitality and the desire to do whatever is necessary to pursue their happiness.

Juan José finished high school and now it is a challenge for us as a family to find opportunities for him to keep studying. In our country, there are no opportunities for young people or adults with autism. It is a fight we have to fight, and we will do it until we get what they need – a place in society, respect and understanding.

I would like to share a photo of him receiving his bachelor's degree, a stage that Juan José enjoyed with friends. He was respected, valued and accepted by his peers.

Finally, I want to leave a message for mothers, fathers, siblings and other family members who read this book: happiness and fulfilment of the dreams of our children with autism are in our hands. We can transform society; we can pave the way; we need only to strengthen ourselves as families and as a collective. And last, but not least, we need to believe in them, in their abilities.

Thanks to Maggi Golding and Jill Stacey for allowing us to participate in this initiative and to tell the whole world that children with autism are the most beautiful gift that God could give us.

Chapter 3

IRENE AND PAMMY

(SOUTH AFRICA)

Pammy was born on 17 January 1974. A big, healthy, and contented baby, two weeks overdue, with a round, beautiful face and lots of hair. The hospital staff had to wake her up to be fed. She was our little moon! She never gave us any trouble with eating or sleeping.

At about three months we got worried about her eyes as they both seemed to squint. We took her to a specialist who, after battling for a long time to examine her, told us that she had a 25 per cent squint in both eyes and that the only way to correct this would be surgery. At six months, she had her first operation on both eyes. For three  weeks, she had to be restrained and her little hands bandaged to stop her from pulling off the bandages on her eyes. It was very traumatic for all of us to see her like that. At 12 months, she had to have the second of five corrective operations, eventually losing the sight in her right eye.

Pammy developed normally, smiling and laughing, and could say mamma and daddy and yaya (granny in Greek), although she refused to walk unaided. About this time, I fell pregnant with my son. At about 18 months we started noticing some changes in her. She stopped responding to us when we talked to her, as if she couldn't hear us, and there was no eye contact. Pammy stopped smiling and played with her little hands in front of her eyes for hours. There was no new communication at all. She never played with toys and threw everything she could lay her hands on. Eventually she started walking unaided (and hasn't stopped ever since). If she wanted something, she would scream.

By 24 months, the screaming and banging of her head on the ground and the walls became a nightmare. We didn't know what to do! The doctor visits started, with assessments of hearing, speech and anything else the doctors could think of. Blood tests, brain scans, x-rays, this medication, that psychiatrist – we went through it all, even the suggestion that she had a brain biopsy, which we refused. We were also told that she would not live beyond 12 years. Nothing prepares you for something as devastating as being told you will lose your child and no doctor can tell you what is wrong. Pammy was also extremely hyperactive, climbing everything, once even hanging with one hand from the railing of our balcony from the 14th floor, all the while screaming and throwing tantrums. We didn't know which way to turn. We lost all our friends and never went out. Even our family found the situation very hard. It put our marriage under a lot of stress, but we decided that this child was given to us by God for a reason and we had better make the best of it.

One of the many doctors we had seen sent us to a paediatrician in Pretoria who apparently specialised in children with the same symptoms, although the term 'autism' was apparently not known to him. Forty years ago, autism in South Africa was not very well known. On 24 December, he called me to his office, sat me down (I was eight months pregnant with my son and had Pammy on my lap), drew his metal wastepaper basket from under his desk and said, 'Mrs Constantinou, your child belongs in here.' Talk about shock! Even today after so many years it makes me very angry. Then he gave me a list of institutions and said goodbye and, 'Good luck, you are going to need it.' There was not a single word of kindness or encouragement for the shocking news he had just given me. I wish I could have taken this child to him and shown him what she has become but he passed away a few years later.

Soon after, I gave birth to a healthy baby boy Mik, petrified that there would be something wrong with him, too. Our next visit was to the new hospital that had just opened in Johannesburg. We saw a young American doctor who finally told us that Pammy was autistic. His advice and recommendations were invaluable. He warned me that it would be an uphill battle and scoffed at the doctor who told me she belongs in an institution. He was so reassuring and kind that I left his room for the first time feeling that there was light at the end of the tunnel. We finally knew what was wrong with our child and that we weren't going to lose her.

Everything started falling into place. Armed with his report we saw our doctor back in Durban, who told us we should contact the Vera School in Cape Town or phone Margaret Golding in Pretoria. A new school was opening in Pretoria and since we had family there, we decided to move there. Pammy was about 4 years old, still in nappies and not communicating. We had even been reported to the child protection services because they thought she

was being abused and we were told to leave our apartment because of her screaming. The more we tried to love her and bond with her, the more she fought us.

Starting the new school was a miracle. The teachers were fantastic. Slowly we started to feel more confident and with the teachers' advice and help we knew what to do at home. One thing Pammy needed was a lot of discipline and routine, otherwise she would scream nonstop. Nappy training was very slow but in the end, at about 5 years old, happiness! Her aggression and lack of communication carried on putting tremendous strain on our marriage and on our little boy. Again, we had no friends as nobody understood our situation. The training, patience and love of her teachers was incredible. She could be such a sweet child. Pammy was put on medication to help her sleep at night (which she fought) and to calm her hyperactivity, but this increased her appetite. She was doing quite well at school and it was recommended that she be a weekly boarder at the Unica Hostel. At first it was very difficult for her to get used to a strange place and she couldn't make friends or get along with the children or teachers. She was always fighting and being very aggressive, but due to her fantastic housemother, Jenny, and all the staff, she eventually settled down. With intense training, lots of love and patience she started talking at about the age of 8. Every new word she said was like heavenly music to us. I remember the first time she was cheeky to me I started dancing around. My baby was actually cheeky to me, and her little smiles made our world sunny again. Unbelievable!

In 1983, I had back surgery and was out of commission for nearly three months, which set her off her routine quite a bit. I would fetch her from boarding school on a Friday and the rest of the weekend we would spend on tenterhooks. Anything would set her off and she would destroy literally everything in her path. Her strength was unbelievable! The only one who could calm her down was her long-suffering and loving little brother. Even the dogs were afraid of her. I admired her teachers at school for their patience and dedication. It couldn't have been easy to be on the receiving end of Pamela's temper. But when she had her very few moments of peace, she was really lovely, helping with chores, playing in the garden with her brother, or just talking to herself.

We had my husband's mother staying with us at that stage, who could not understand why her grandchild was like this. You try and explain to a Greek granny how difficult bringing a child up with autism is going to be, and that what she knew about parenting was going to be a bit different. Pammy and her Greek granny clashed all the time. Then puberty came along. What a nightmare! She started putting on weight slowly, then depression reared its ugly head. Menstruation became a huge problem, as she started at about 10 years old. We had to hide anything that was sharp, and she would climb the gate and stand with her arms stretched out in front of oncoming traffic, or climb the six-foot fence and walk on it as if it was the pavement. Breaking things around the house was a favourite pastime, and fighting with mother was another one. I cannot remember how many times she told me she hated me and that she would run away. I actually packed her bags many times and told her to go.

Hugging her at that stage was out of the question, as was eye contact. At around 15 years of age, a school psychologist recommended she have a hysterectomy to help with the menstruation problem. That was heartbreaking for us. There had always been that hope that eventually, by some miracle, everything would be normal and she could go ahead and have a normal life with someone and have children, but this really was a wake-up call to us as parents. We had accepted long ago that she was autistic, but we never stopped dreaming. Lots of red tape later, she had the operation and her appendix was removed at the same time. The nurses at the hospital couldn't get enough of her. She was their best patient and they spoilt her rotten for the week she was there. Slowly, Pammy started calming down a bit, being a bit more affectionate, able to dress herself and communicate better, although we still had an occasional adult meltdown. She slowly came off all her medication.

At the age of 16, Pammy left Unica School because we decided to move back to Umhlanga Rocks near Durban, where we opened a bakery. As there were no autistic schools in Durban, she attended the Golden Hours School and did very well. She made quite a few friends. That is when she started taking her weight seriously, swimming until she looked like a prune, taking long walks on the beach, entering any race possible and still pulling our poor little Maltese poodle Bella along, her feet not touching the ground. This child was a totally different human. Much calmer, friendlier, and more affectionate, she would also come and help at the bakery. She knew every customer by name and had quite a following!

When the National Lottery first started, we got a machine installed. Pammy was handling the machine, issuing tickets and giving change with no mistakes. God help anyone who said she made a mistake! Our customers said she was their lucky charm and wanted to be served only by her.

We did occasionally have our famous mother/daughter wars, but with my son and his heavy metal guitar obsession at the time, we could scream at each other with the poor neighbours thinking it was him! Religion has always played a very big part in our lives. When Pammy was 4, we had taken her to the Living Waters healing line. As she grew up and started understanding more, she joined the church youth group and her faith became stronger and stronger. It is very strong now. She started doing little arts and crafts, making beautiful cards out of dry flowers and houses out of ice cream sticks and tissue boxes. She loved being creative and made lots of Christmas presents. She even taught herself Italian from a phrase book. One day, a customer of ours offered to teach her embroidery, or candlewicking as it is called. She made two double bedspreads and cushions for her bedroom. It took her four years to finish but she was so proud of herself.

As Pammy got older she started noticing that she was different and so started questioning what was wrong with her. We would have long conversations about autism. I always believed in discipline and I have always been strict with her because I wanted a child who could be as sociable and as independent as possible and that is why we never went anywhere without her. We wanted to expose her to the world as much as possible! She would go up to people and introduce herself with a smile on her face. It was heartbreaking sometimes for us to see how people reacted to her and not be able to do something to make her feel better. She is not at all shy nowadays in the company of others.

At the age of 19, she had to leave Golden Hours School and she started attending the Challenge Ltd workshop daily, where she stayed for eight years. In the beginning, Pammy was happy, but as time went by it was not challenging enough for her. She made a few friends, with whom she is still in contact today. Her special male friend, Allan, moved to New Zealand and that was a bit of a knock. Sadly, he passed away about six years ago, but they used to phone and send little parcels to each other. He was her 'boyfriend' and when he died she was very upset. Over the years, she has lost some of her friends and favourite members of her family and while she always showed her emotions, she is very realistic about death. She even comforts the adults. Pammy has always been kind and caring towards other people. At one stage, she had about ten penpals and was very involved in their lives. One penpal, who was in jail, took advantage of her good heart for a long time and it took me a long while to get her out of this situation.

Pammy used to do all the banking for our bakery business

and although the bakery has closed, I am still baking from home. Pammy now phones my customers for orders, as well as doing the payments to the suppliers for my ingredients. She makes her own bed, cleans her room, polishes her shoes, takes the dog for a walk, goes to the supermarket for shopping, and sometimes washes the dishes – everything that she would have to do if I was not around. One thing she cannot do is shop for clothes and shoes, although this is an ongoing lesson. Anything that fits her, even if it is ten sizes too big, and an ugly colour, she says, 'It's lovely, Mom!' Looking in the mirror had not been one of her favourite things, but now she looks into one all the time.

About 12 years ago, we moved to Cape Town to be closer to my son. He and Pammy have always had a close and loving relationship. Pammy blossomed in Cape Town. We opened a coffee shop and she would sometimes come and serve the customers, who loved her gentle and smiley face. Because of the long hours we worked, she took over the running of the household, and of course still made poor Bella, the dog, fly behind her. We also have a bird that Pammy cleans and reprimands if it makes a mess. She collected the bird's feathers over the years and has made a beautiful picture of it.

A few years ago, my father died in Greece and my mother came to live with us. We have a two-bedroom apartment and Pammy's room had to be given to granny. Pammy had to sleep on the couch in the lounge, which made her very unhappy. A year later, granny had a major operation and two days afterwards had a massive stroke, taking her speech and understanding away. She had rehabilitation for a long time. It was a very difficult time for all of us, but especially Pamela. Nothing prepares you for the difficulty of looking after a very dependant person. Pammy used to take my mother out for a walk every day and was adamant about her granny being able to keep as mobile as possible. Slowly, granny started being dependant on her wheelchair. I would not have been able to look after my mother if my daughter had not been there. As difficult as it must have been for her, and tears would sometimes flow (from both of us) out of frustration, Pammy was unbelievably strong, all the time saying we should trust God for help. She would take her granny out every day in the wheelchair, pushing her along so that granny's hair would fly behind her and she had a permanent smile on her face. To make granny feel calm when we put her to bed at night, Pammy would act like a clown to make her laugh and give her lots and lots of kisses before we tucked her in. When my mother passed away three years later, Pammy was very sad but very relieved that her suffering was finally over. A lot of lessons were learned by both of us in that period. She moved back to her bedroom, which is now a garden of flowers and butterflies, with more being added every day.

Pammy might have taken a long time to walk, but she hasn't stopped since. She has dozens of medals from all her races, ranging from 5k to 21k. She still walks daily, an average of 6k, while reading a book and holding a cup of coffee (a feat no healthy human can achieve), and hikes as often as possible. She even leads some hikes. She has always been good at arithmetic and was even able to work out in her mind when she was conceived! She remembers everyone's birthdays and the year they were born. If we want to know something that happened 20 years ago, we say, 'Ask our Google.' Her memory is fantastic.

Since she could write, she has kept a diary. Over the years, they have amounted to about 30 of all sizes, and numerous pieces of paper. Three years ago, she decided to rewrite them all and has also remembered certain forgotten details. Between writing and making crafts she has kept very busy. She has made lovely pictures for her room and displayed them with great pride. I have also made Pammy my official housekeeper. She makes a list at the end of the month of what is needed in the house, I give her the money and she does the shopping, making sure she gets the best prices and keeps up to date with all the specials.

About five years ago, she joined the Hillsong Church, which is very near us. Over the years, she has done a lot of volunteering, going to a physically handicapped school and a primary school, helping with Bible lessons, chatting and playing with the kids. On Sundays, she helps in the clothing section of the church for two or three hours. Her faith is very strong, and she reads her Bible every day. She helps anyone who asks for her help, as she is very empathetic. Unfortunately, she is sometimes taken advantage of! Today's world overwhelms her in its brutality and nastiness. Three years ago, my husband had a heart attack and a stroke. Although he cannot drive anymore, he has gone back to work. We have to keep a close eye on him, which his daughter does with great pleasure, pushing him to do exercise, eat properly, take his medication, and telling him she wants him around for a long time. And he absolutely adores his princess!

As a woman, she now likes to have her hair dyed, wears lipstick, likes nice clothes (which, of course, I have to pick), and likes to look into every mirror and say, 'I am gorgeous.' I never go into her room to clean. She keeps everything in order and likes the flat to be clean and tidy. Strict routine is very important to her. One thing I have not been able to do is to replace our dog. She won't even think about it. I think she had enough of dragging our poor old doggie behind her for 17 years. I believe an animal would have been good for her, but I couldn't force the issue.

She has become very affectionate and loving, wanting hugs and kisses and telling me and her dad she loves us, all the time. She now loves reading books, sending lots of WhatsApp messages, and talking on the phone to her friends. She hardly ever watches TV as she says that sometimes she cannot understand what they are talking about. She would rather read a book or write in her diary. She always wants to learn new things but struggles on the computer. She likes going for coffee or a milkshake alone, and loves going out for dinner. Beach visits are a highlight, as she still loves the water. She is very slim, even though she has a very sweet tooth and a good appetite and fights with her father over chocolates that I have to hide.

The one thing she still questions is why people don't have long conversations with her. It breaks my heart to have to explain why, as she is so clever and functions very highly. Although her speech is good, her communication skills are still not understood by many. Loud noise, too many people and a break in her routine still stress her, but she tries very hard to cope.

Sometimes we cannot believe that this is the same child we were blessed with 42 years ago. Pammy has come such a long way and through her sheer determination is what she is today. Her smile and loving nature are things we would never imagine possible. She has impeccable manners and is always clean and tidy herself. About five years ago, she even travelled to the UK alone to join her brother for three weeks, and has now become an aunty to Liam, who she adores. She is always on the go and looking for ways to help people. She has become an incredible young woman, loving her birthdays as she says she becomes wiser at each passing year. Never mind the grey hair. We are so proud of who she is today, and we call her our miracle child and thank God for her every day. She has made our marriage stronger and brought us closer together as a family.

I know that when I'm not around anymore she will not be a burden to her brother or to anyone else. Cooking is something she will not venture into as she is afraid of getting burnt, but she makes a mean salad and killer sandwiches. She will always need some form of support in her day-to-day life and help with her finances, but she will cope. As long as she keeps that wonderful smile on her face and her never-give-up attitude, all will be well.

The journey has been long and sometimes heartbreaking. As a mother, you cannot bear to see your child in such a state and wonder if you could have done something more to help her. Your confidence is shattered and sometimes you blame yourself. Did I do something wrong while I was pregnant? Was it my fault in any way? Could I have done something to prevent this? So many questions. You know that somewhere in there is a very special person but you just don't know how to bring it out. Today, that very special person has appeared in leaps and bounds.

Sometimes, a friend will say something innocent that stabs you in the heart, but you just carry on, because if you take everything personally your life will become bitter. You have to be consistent, disciplined and loving. Lots of patience and humour are essential requirements or you will start banging your head against the wall. Never give up hope that sunshine will come back into your life.

Having Pammy has been my life journey. I have learned many lessons from her along the way. Being a very young mother, I had to grow up very fast. And I realised that without the help, love and support of my family, especially my sister who is also Pammy's godmother, I would not have been able to make this journey! My husband and I had a little angel, closed-up and uncommunicative, who has now spread her wings wide and is touching so many lives.

Daddy and I are so proud of you Pammy, and love you so much!

Chapter 4

ISABEL AND DAVID

(SPAIN)

It seems beneficial to start listening to parents of people with autism. It is important that you know about our experience, our hope, anguish and the great mix of emotions. We have a combination of sadness, joy, anguish and uncertainty about the future of our children. In my case, I started over 40 years ago in this 'fight'. I realise that we have advanced in many ways, but the question still remains as to what will happen when our children with autism are older and we are gone.

My name is Isabel Bayonas – mother of David, who is a person with autism. Forty years ago, virtually nothing was known about autism. There were no specialised professionals and often the misdiagnoses of 'subnormal', 'crazy' or 'deaf' were given. My son David did not receive a diagnosis of autism until he was nearly 10 years old. In his case, the diagnosis was said to be intellectual impairment with an IQ (intelligence quotient) of 65.

David did not start walking until he was 18 months and did not speak until the age of 9, when he began to use single words such as 'water' and 'bread'. He was a hyperactive child who, since he had been a few months old, had been regularly self-injurious, biting his index finger, biting and hitting himself hard on the head, as well as waving and flapping his arms as he spun around screaming.

Several diagnoses were made during those years and none of them matched. When David was 5, a doctor told me that he would never be able to do basic things for himself, such as dressing and eating, and he would never read and write. At that time, the least thing that worried me was that he may never read and write – what I really wanted was for my son to be happy and content. This doctor specifically advised me to place David in a psychiatric hospital. I will not go into everything I've been through because all families have probably had similar experiences, but what I do want to say to other families is that all is never lost and you should always strive for improvement. I promised myself that my child would never live in a mental hospital and, despite what that doctor said about his future, that together David and I would prove he was capable of a lot more.

When David was 11 years old, I increasingly became aware that there would never be a cure for autism and that it was something that would be part of our lives forever. I decided that we must aim for David's full potential and above all, for him to be happy. So, I set to work to that end. With the help of my other sons and his father, neighbours and others who knew David, we were able to achieve all that David is today: a happy person. What I mean by this is that there is always hope. Although my son does have an intellectual disability as well as his autism, he has a very strong family, is socially well integrated and happy.

I have recently focused on work with the aim to promote

self-determination. When I say 'David, you have to decide,' he answers, 'So, what is it?' Then I sit down with him and try to explain what it is that needs to be decided and then he will say, 'Now I understand.' When I buy clothes, for example, he comes with me and he decides which shirt or pants he wants. When he takes his new clothes home, he is happy and proudly says, 'I have chosen them for me.' It is important that you ask children with autism their opinion and teach them that they can decide for themselves.

In the neighbourhood where we live, everyone knows and loves David. I taught him to go to buy bread, and the newspaper, and spent three months teaching him to be able to catch the bus on his own. David visually understands situations very well, so I showed him the numbers of the bus stops where he needed to get on and off the bus, with the result that he now travels alone on the bus.

With some support, David works at the neighbourhood news-stand. It is an activity that helps him to be involved in the community. He visually recognises all the different newspapers and so, when a person asks for a specific newspaper, he can give the correct one.

For families, in general, it is always very important to ensure good communication channels, and in the case of families with an autistic person, it is vital. You need to share problems, talk to the brothers and sisters to explain the situation, ask for their understanding and support, as well as let them know that, above all, they should treat their brother or sister with autism respectfully and in a manner as normal as possible. If a sibling is younger they can teach him to play, to interact, to imitate. If a sibling is older, they should try not to over-protect their younger sibling with autism. Encouraging siblings to explain autism to their friends helps them to include their autistic sibling in activities with their friends. While encouraging the involvement of brothers and sisters, parents need to be careful not to overload them with too much responsibility. As a family unit, responsibilities do need to be shared, but we must also remember the challenges and difficult times our other children will face as a result of their autistic sibling.

All families need a stable and quiet family environment, but more so for a person with autism and we must do our utmost to fully integrate the autistic son or daughter equally into the family. I believe our family has achieved this and it is something I am very happy about and proud of. My other children want and love their brother, and are endlessly teaching him new things, without being over-protective.

It is important to involve the person with autism in housework, for instance making their bed, setting the table, drying the dishes, sweeping the garden, buying the bread, all of which David does in our home. It is something that will provide a sense of achievement and self-worth, which will make that person very happy. We found this approach stopped self-injurious behaviours, reduced hyperactivity and made David more sociable, polite and capable of self-control. Over time, I have managed David's integration into the neighbourhood. People know him, love him and also feel part of his achievements. Sometimes they say to me, 'Lady Bayonas, how David has improved! We are getting there.' Is that not too beautiful?

I believe that every family and every government must take into account that children with autism have the right to:

- free medical and health care
- respect and acceptance in their family
- adequate integration in school, with professionals trained specifically for autism
- respect as citizens
- integration into the environment where they live

- understanding of how they are and acceptance of the peculiarities of their behaviour
- work, to the best of their ability
- functional activities, to motivate them and make sense to them
- transition to adulthood treatment
- happiness.

Whatever it takes, we all need to work together: families, professionals and society. We should all try to understand and know their world. We spend our lives trying to get these children to understand and adapt to us, but what do we know and understand of their world? Our children with autism are special, yes, they are different, and like us, they have strengths and weaknesses. They can provide a lot of joy and satisfaction, like everyone else. We have to work day to day to make them as independent as possible and, most importantly, enable them to be happy.

I've worked with my family for over 40 years to ensure happiness for David, and now it is he who makes us happy! David accompanies me to many conferences each year. Once he gave a talk in Madrid to Complutense University students in psychology and speech therapy. He also came with me to Colombia and Mexico. As David cannot read,  for the conference, I prepared pictograms, so he could be reminded of what he wanted to tell the audience. At such conferences, David talks about what we do every day at home, at work, and so on, and when it finishes, he asks me if he did well!

It is important to explain to David so that he knows ahead of time what activities are expected to occur that day, where we will be going and what we will be doing, thus giving him predictability and peace of mind.

We must also be careful about what we say when our children with autism are present, because we can underestimate their ability to understand what we are saying, but also, they may misinterpret what we are saying. I speak slowly to David, in short, simple sentences and try to establish visual contact. Sometimes it amazes me that some things I thought he had not understood after a while he reminds me of! So, we should not assume that some things are not understood.

Since David's diagnosis, I have spent a lot of time fighting for the rights of people with autism and I have been active in community movements. In 1976, along with other parents, I founded the first association of parents of people with autism of Spain, called APNA (Asociación de Padres de Personas con Autismo).

In 1982, I was a founding member of CERMI, the Spanish Committee of Representatives of People with Disabilities. The Spanish Federation of Parents and/or Guardians of People with Autism (FESPAU) was founded in 1994. In 1998, I was a founding member of the World Autism Organisation and in 1999, I was part of the American Federation of Autism. In short, my life has been focused on fighting to improve the situation of people who, like David, have autism. He has been the engine that has kept me going to do all those things and more. I made a promise to God that part of my life and my time would be devoted to other children like David, and other mothers like me. I have taken 42 years working on that promise. It is wonderful to be able to help other families overcome their problems and show them that all is not lost, to help them see that what David and I have achieved emphasises that we must have strength and confidence and not give up. We have the right and obligation to do so.

One day I asked David if he was happy. He answered yes, which is heartwarming because we all love him. For me, that is my greatest achievement.

Chapter 5

JACKIE AND JOEY

(USA)

I look at my Joey now, 22 years old, smiling, happy. I think back to my innocent baby. He was my first baby but not the first baby in the family. My sister Mary Lou had two kids: my nephew Henry and my niece Mary Kate. Henry was 3 when Joey was born, and Mary Kate was 1. When Mary Kate was born we had a little scare. I was pregnant with Joey at the time and the doctors thought she might be convulsing. They ordered a spinal tap and, luckily, she was all clear – she was just a really strong crier! I couldn't wait for Joey to join his cousins – what fun we all would have!

My husband Joe and I had purchased a small house on Long Island near the beach and hoped to spend the next few years slowly fixing it up. It would be a great place to escape from the city and would be good for all the kids and our new baby on the way.

'Joey, make the sad face again', we used to say. So began our journey into the world of autism. My 14-month-old baby boy was having myoclonic head drops. Seizures in babies don't always look like you might have expected; I thought he was playing a game. My mom and sisters thought differently. It was suggested I video the 'sad face' and show the doctors. We didn't have video cameras on our phones then, so I took videos on a giant camera, with tapes and took them to a neurologist who suggested an electro-encephalogram (EEG) to see if they were seizures. I vividly

remember getting the phone call on my cell phone, also a giant contraption at the time, from the doctor suggesting that my husband and I come in for the results. I walked out of a meeting with a bunch of executives to take the call; I knew it couldn't be good if he wanted us to come in.

From that moment on began the quest to figure out what was wrong with Joey. Why was he having seizures? I quit my job as vice president of a textile company and became a consultant. We moved from our little studio apartment in New York City to the semi-wreck of a house on Long Island, thinking services would be better there. We spent years eliminating horrible diseases and genetic disorders, all the while trying to get the seizures to stop – there were dozens of them daily, four or five clusters of 10 to 25 head drops every day. Side effects from medication and, we would later learn, autism, were taking our beautiful little boy away.

At one point, prednisone was suggested to stop the seizures. Joey gained so much weight and became so aggressive that my husband would have to dress in several layers of thick clothing at night to try and get Joey to sleep. He fought my husband off each night, scratching and biting in a drug-fuelled rage. It was awful. My poor parents often stayed with us to help. It was heartbreaking to watch. My young niece and nephew were a joy; they didn't care what Joey did. They could sense he was different but loved him just the same.

'We'd like to try Joey in the ABA class we are starting', said the director of his early intervention, centre-based, preschool. ABA stands for applied behaviour analysis. It's been found to help teach kids with autism. Autism? I wondered. Who has autism? Our son has a seizure disorder. We had established that there are no epilepsy schools and that many autistic children have seizures. Joey was 2.5 years old, taking a little school bus every day to preschool, still having seizures all day, drooling and putting everything in his mouth. Each day I followed the bus to and from the school. When he wasn't having a seizure, he was running around, endlessly spinning and whirling, reaching and grabbing. He was not toilet trained and no longer spoke. He had been counting in both English and Spanish and always asking, 'What's that?' 'Who's that?'

Joey turned 4 and his seizures had become part of our life. We had eliminated all known diseases and conditions that could be causing them, had tried every known traditional medicine available, alternative medicines, diets, treatment within reason, and maybe beyond reason. We had begun to accept that maybe they would never go away and that we would just have to make the best life possible for him. At that point, I was pregnant with baby number two. I still needed to be in the hospital with Joey for yet another overnight EEG, in a twin bed with Joey tethered to a machine by 32 leads he did *not* want to keep on his head. I realised that this poor kid never did anything fun, that his life was about therapy, doctor visits and school. I thought there must be classes for special kids like him. I promised him that some day he was going to have fun like other kids, laugh and play, and that life was more than hospitals and medicines and special diets.

It's a boy – another boy! We didn't know then what we know now – that the likelihood of my second son being on the spectrum was double the rate than the general population. Even ignorant of those facts, I was completely paranoid, watching for a seizure every two minutes. I paged the head of neurology twice while in the hospital after delivery, convinced the baby was having myoclonic jerks. Luckily, he was only really crying. He was our little Andrew, and it was a miracle to witness typical development!

When Joey was 5 it was time to move to a regular school-age programme and we needed to classify our child with a disability in order to receive services. In New York, you have to select a disability from a list you wish you'd never seen. At the time, autism was not even on the list. We went with 'other health impaired', as speech delay didn't really cover all that was happening with Joey. Again, I followed the school bus, but this time the school placement was so far away that I would stick around all day, nearby in case he had a bad seizure, so I could get there quickly.

Joey's seizures started getting worse. They evolved into drop seizures, where with no warning, he just dropped and fell over. He needed a helmet for safety.

Shortly after Andrew was born, my father was diagnosed with leukaemia and he passed away in February 2000. We were devastated. Then, incredibly, Joey's seizures stopped, just as we were exploring surgery to insert a vagus nerve stimulator. It was bizarre the way they just stopped. We had cranked up his medication to adult doses as a last-ditch effort before an invasive procedure, and they stopped. No one could explain it – my father died, and Joey's seizures stopped.

A whole new world without seizures! We took a couple of years to absorb this as we planned to lower medication, but the timing was uncertain. It was so unusual that they had stopped, and we were so fearful they would return. Perhaps now he would be able to learn? Maybe now he would talk? Calm down? With less medication and side effects and without his brain being interrupted all day, maybe progress could be made? Maybe he could be toilet trained now?

We moved back to New York City when Joey was 7 and Andrew was 3. We didn't want to be separated again like we were on 9/11, when both of us were in the city that fateful day. Joey's school choices on Long Island had really narrowed; there were no schools purely with ABA for autism, and no schools in our district for kids like Joey. There was one school, and that was the only choice – a school for kids with various types of disability or ability, as I like to think. It seemed to me that this was not the best idea. All these kids have unique needs, and to throw them all together and work on arts and crafts all day seemed like giving up. He was only 7. We moved to a place across the street from where Joey was born in New York City. (Try telling people that right after 9/11 you are moving *back* into New York City!) I lost my consulting job eight months later, but Joey's seizures had stopped, so life was different. Unfortunately, we couldn't find a school in New York City either; public school was not an option, so there were only very expensive private schools. Parents needed to sue the Board of Education to be reimbursed for the tuition. While looking for a school, we hired private therapists to retain some sort of structure for Joey, but the monthly bill was astronomical for such an 'a la carte' programme.

Poor Andrew, I was so preoccupied with Joey that I forgot the nightmare of New York City school admissions! You have to be on a list practically while the child is in utero. Fortunately, Andrew was accepted at school where he made friends and the invitations started rolling in to join a sports class, learn to ice skate, and go to birthday parties.

I remembered the hospital stay when I realised Joey needed to start to have fun. In the interim, we found a school for him, a state-approved school so we didn't have to sue. I then began to look for a special needs after-school programme, but we were rejected because Joey was not toilet trained at the age of 7, had a history of seizures and had additional behaviour needs they could not support.

Where do you go when you are rejected from the special needs class? I decided to do it myself. I said to my husband, 'I think I need to start something.' So, I rented a place, worked with people who helped with Joey's home programme and created 'snack' – the Special Needs Activity Center for Kids.

We started snack by renting a facility for two hours on Friday after school. We hired an ABA therapist, an art teacher, a music teacher and two teaching assistants, most from special needs schools. Those early classes taught us a lot and we got good at giving these kids a chance to learn how to participate while addressing their needs. Soon we added another group, then we moved to a larger space. The need for a programme like ours was huge. Our programme was created for the kids who had challenging behaviours, who bit kids, or banged their heads, who could not or would not talk, who were not toilet trained. We had no intake, so *no one* would be turned away, as Joey had been. The person in charge of behaviour would do an evaluation and train the staff person assigned with strategies to help kids succeed in the programme. It was sad to see that so many parents fibbed about their children's behaviour on our application form, claiming out of fear of being rejected that there were no challenging behaviours to report.

We developed a two-hour class with the help of therapists – movement, snack time, music and art – in four, 30-minute segments. No group was larger than six – with a minimum of two kids per staff and a lead in each speciality, all overseen by a behaviour therapist. The fees were similar to those at typical children's programmes. All staff were hired and trained, so the kids had the consistency they needed. Volunteers could be peer models. Parents could drop-off. Programming was designed and staffed for success. Then we added a swim programme, involving one-to-one swim classes where only our kids were in the pool to help alleviate the sensory issues of sounds and smells. Boys could be helped with changing by their mums in a family changing area. Most importantly, families were made to feel comfortable if their child had a meltdown, or had a toileting accident in the pool. Next, we added sports such as soccer classes, so all could succeed, and dads could take their boys to soccer rather than therapy. A holiday programme came next, with classes all day when schools were on break. As the kids got older, we added teen programming and then eventually added an asterisk to our logo to denote snack* – Special Needs Activity Centre for Kids and *Adults.

It was not as easy as this summary of the last 15 years makes it sound. We poured so much of our money into this project as we realised at that point, a cure for Joey and others his age may elude them. We believed it was critical to start a programme that directly touched the kids and helped families have some respite, gave the kids some opportunity to practise all they were learning in their rigorous therapies and a chance to be with other kids. It became clear if snack* was to be able to continue with the quality our kids so deserved, we would need to start to fundraise, to fund the gap between the cost of the programme and the revenue the fees generated. It was important to us that there was a fee schedule because people need to have skin in the game, as they say. If we awarded a total scholarship, attendance could be erratic, which is not beneficial, but we couldn't charge what it really cost to run our classes as no one would be able to afford it. We knew all too well about that as we had previously had huge bills to pay from private therapies. So, we charged fees similar to what Andrew's programmes cost as we did not want there to be a disability surcharge due to the small class size and high ratio of staff to kids.

Autism Speaks was founded around the same time as snack*. It was doing a great job with its mission of raising awareness and funding research. It had enveloped the other grassroot organisations that had formed in response to the huge number of kids being diagnosed. The Autism Speaks Walk began, and I remember attending the first one on Long Island in Eisenhower Park. I was overwhelmed at the sheer number of families, families like ours, including the now familiar tell-tale signs of youngsters with autism – flapping, tantrums, hands over their ears, beautiful kids mostly boys, all like our boy. There were people as far as the eye could see. The sight of so many affected kids and families overwhelmed me as much as it made me feel we were certainly not alone. As we were walking, a buzz began in the crowd and soon word got to us – a child, one of the autistic children, was missing. In no time at all, many of the mothers who knew the park layout started running to the lake. Lo and behold there was the boy in the middle of the lake. So many of the kids, as most mums knew, had an unhealthy fascination with water. He was fine – but we were all shaken to the core.

Once word got out that snack* was the place for challenging kids, parents became so much more relaxed knowing we would not ask a child to leave the programme for having needs that were too intense. We had difficult parents maybe, but not kids!

Soon we had the snack three-week rule. The first three weeks were a rough transition, but once a kid knew we understood them, they actually looked forward to coming and got into sync with the group. Parents had a chance to go and read a book or meet other parents and hang out to learn from each other while their kids were being safely engaged. The best things we ever learned about schools, therapies, doctors, lawyers and programmes have all come from other parents. Joe and I have thoroughly enjoyed the bonus of meeting other parents like us.

We added more days of programmes and more staff. Today we serve close to 200 kids, teens and adults per week with swimming lessons, sports classes, music, art and cooking segments. We run all day when there are school holidays as we know our kids don't do well with that much downtime; they need to be engaged and they don't need time to practise being autistic.

The teen years were probably the most traumatic of all. I do not want to frighten other mothers, but you must be prepared. For typically developing children, the teen years are usually a time of tremendous growth filled with new social opportunities, greater independence and integration into larger society. For children with developmental disabilities like autism, entering adolescence often has the reverse effect. Rather than their world expanding, their bigger physical size and the frequent increase in their challenging behaviours often lead to a more restrictive existence than when they were younger children.

There were several aggressive episodes that occurred as Joey reached puberty. He was on very little medication, giving his poor liver a break from having been on meds since he was 14 months old until we began to lower his meds at the age of 10. When he was about 14 years old, we changed schools for Joey as the Department of Education in its infinite wisdom would not grant an age expansion to his public-funded school. We were offered a spot at the Westchester campus, which, even with no traffic, is a good one- to two-hour ride from our apartment. Not a great offer for a boy on a toileting schedule of 30 minutes, who is non-verbal with a history of seizures, and has aggressive, self-injurious behaviour emerging. Once again, we took matters into our hands and placed him in a private school well-known for its good management of adolescence. We sued and won reimbursement for the high-priced tuition.

Early in the transition, Andrew had a day off from school and Joey didn't. I thought Andrew and I would drive Joey to school and then run errands. As I merged onto the FDR Drive, I noticed Joey was starting to whine a bit and the next thing I knew, he was pulling my hair as I was driving. He was biting his wrists and drawing blood and Andrew, who was sitting next to him, was understandably hysterical. By the grace of God, I was able to get off at the 23rd exit – eerily close to Bellevue Hospital. Andrew had hopped into the front passenger seat and was begging me to call the police. I called the school and 911 – I had no plan. I put Andrew on the sidewalk, opened the sunroof and locked Joey in the car. I was covered in blood when the police arrived already equipped with gloves as if they were wrangling a bear. I refused to unlock the car until the cops heard me out. I screamed, 'Do you boys have mothers? Well, I am this boy's mother and I need you to calm down,' to which they replied, 'Well, you called us lady!' I told them it would all go a lot better if they calmed down and let me and Andrew ride in the ambulance with Joey to the hospital. Joey would only get in the ambulance if was I with him. We left my car where it was for friends to collect later.

The emergency room didn't know what to do and placed a huge guard outside Joey's bedroom. Luckily, Joey was not yet 16.5, otherwise they would have admitted him to the adult psych ward without my permission. Thus, began our introduction to psychotropic drugs and the new horrors of living with side effects such as weight gain, incontinence, hair loss and the post-traumatic stress of waiting for these rages to reappear. I won't lie by telling you that the ages 14 to 19 were not rough years. We did discover that Joey had impacted wisdom teeth during this time, which certainly didn't help. These impacted teeth could not be seen without an x-ray and he only had x-rays under anaesthesia. It helped when that issue was resolved, but we still periodically have bouts of what we call 'Saturday Night at the Fights' though not as intense and not as often as that first one. Joey still takes anti-seizure medication and we hope maybe to remove the psychotics altogether some day.

My Joey is 22 now and so are many of those first kids who came to snack*. Those who have not gone on to a residential school placement are all joining Joey as they take adult classes at snack*. When we started our teen programming, we added a pre-vocational aspect, inviting local special needs schools to bring their students to job sample. We set  up different stations for shredding paper, counting inventory and packing up items for shipping, to give kids in school a chance to practise different jobs to see what might be a good fit. For some, just leaving school was a challenge. We then started a business – an e-commerce site selling cosmetics and coffee. An odd pairing, I know, but two things I could source. The kids learn to take an inventory, label, ship, make an order, and so on. This project has now grown to be a part of our adult programme. Our members make their own decisions as regards their schedule and thus what classes they attend. We provide music, technology, exercise and cooking, to name a few.

The state provides funds to parents and members to hire their own community habitation worker who can accompany their children to assist, if needed, with participation in the class. This way, these members have the best of all with the option of choice and freedom yet a group experience. They take trips to museums, movies and other recreational places together as they are part of a community with their own versions of friendships.

Life is full for Joey, and he is happy most of the time. Andrew is going to college and we now will focus on where Joey will live on his own. Who will care for him besides his brother and cousins? Joey has had two seizures in the past two years. Will his intense seizures return? Will he be able to live and eventually die in peace?

My role as a mother has changed since Joey was born in 1995. We are close – we are simpatico. I've become part lawyer, doctor, advocate and fundraiser, for more than just my two boys, more than for my family, but for people I never knew I'd meet, people I never knew would become such an important part of my everyday life. The future is unknown, but we face what we must. We don't have a choice.

Chapter 6

JILL AND MICHAEL

(SOUTH AFRICA)

'Now this is a rare sight – your son's eyes are wide open like a bush baby's,' said the obstetrician after he pulled my first born, a boy, from my womb during an epidural caesarean. I should have known then this could well have been a warning sign for what my future might bring!

We named our first son Michael, and off we launched into parenthood!

Sleep was a rarity in the first year of Michael's life. When Michael fed off the breast, he either gulped litres or refused to take anything. Weaning him onto solids was a troublesome time, with him gagging and spitting out the food, which I thought was my cooking, but was later to learn it was due to sensory issues.

I attended a 'mums and toddlers' group, which was socially enjoyable, but emotionally hard as I realised as time went by that Michael was somehow just not the same as the others and slightly delayed on the milestones. Although nothing was said to me at these tea afternoons, I sometimes felt that the other parents, despite being very friendly, wondered what I had done wrong in my pregnancy, or what I might be doing wrong as a parent. And, of course, there was one professional on a mission to try and identify the causes of the behaviours and delays, who asked whether Michael had ever been the victim of abuse.

Remember that all this was happening from 1984 to 1986, when hardly any clinicians knew anything about autism, and so my concerns were dismissed. Also, prior to giving birth I had just qualified as a registered nurse and midwife, so not only was I expected to cope, but when I started suspecting something was wrong with Michael, I was told I was a 'neurotic nursing sister mother'.

At the age of 2 years, Michael was enrolled in a playschool. This lasted two months before I was asked to remove him as he was pushing other children and not listening to instructions.

A special needs teacher who had started her own playgroup offered to take Michael, and despite the fact I dreaded the phone ringing in the morning when he was at the playgroup, this was successful for the ensuing year. During this time, the teacher also noticed that Michael was not 'quite right' and suggested I took him for an assessment, which I duly did.

The outcome was a diagnosis of 'minimal brain dysfunction with speech delay' and Michael started receiving speech therapy and occupational therapy at a school for children with cerebral palsy. Michael was then admitted as a full-time pupil at this school, which went well for two years until more verbal instruction was involved. I got a call one morning to say that Michael had destroyed the 'conversation area' of the classroom and this was basically the last straw after they had done their best to accommodate him in the school – albeit without ever beginning to really understand his behaviours and his total lack of speech.

During these years, I had supportive friends, one of whom had bought me a book about a mother's struggles with an autistic child. My friend bought this book as she knew the life I was living with Michael, but had no idea about autism, let alone that this was what he might have – fate works in mysterious ways! Coincidentally, I was on the first chapter when I received the call from the school saying he could not come back to the school after the end of the term. I dug back into this book to escape the situation, only to find I was turning the pages more and more rapidly as my son's life started to appear on each page. 'My goodness, I think Michael has autism.' I searched my nursing files and found a 'checklist for possible autism' and he scored 15 out of 18 points.

The school was unsure what autism was and did not know any schools for autism, so being left unaided, without the internet and good old Google in those days, I got out the telephone book, where I eventually found a school for children with autism in Johannesburg. After an assessment, the school accepted my beautiful little redheaded 5-year-old and here started our pathway into the world of autism.

I was devastated by the diagnosis, though so relieved to eventually know what was wrong with Michael and that, therefore, there was a way forwards. At that point, obviously, we did not have a true idea as to how severe Michael's autism and intellectual impairment really were, which perhaps in a way acted to soften the blow of the diagnosis. I went through a long, hard, desperately sad time, feeling lost and lonely. As Michael settled into the correct educational setting, and I, for the first time, met parents with children like Michael, those long weeks of experiencing sorrow each and every day, started turning into weeks where I had six sad days and one decent day, and over time became six pretty good days and one bad day. I admit it took me ages to agree to attend the school's support group and once I did, I was sorry I had not done so beforehand!

Michael was now in an environment where people understood him, and people accepted me, a mother who had not done something wrong. We moved house to be nearer the school, I had a beautiful daughter and an even keel seemed to be appearing. The school was in dire financial straits, so I became their fundraiser and the doors of the school remained open (not without many bumps) thanks to great donors, a fundraising committee and staff.

I became further involved in the field of autism, starting the full-time offices of Autism South Africa and remaining National Director for over 20 years. During this time, I repeatedly noticed how the age of the child with autism, and thus their stage in the path of acceptance and adaptation, significantly affected the parents' response to advice and the actions they undertook. Once you or others notice that your child is 'different', denial and no action are prominent, and often this is around the age of 1–3 years. Moving on to 3–7 years, when really you can no longer dismiss or ignore the worrying aspects that are present before you in your child, 'dramatic' action comes into play. This is when, as I most certainly did, parents start seeking all types of advice, rushing around buying every educational toy they can lay their hands on, seeking alternative and often highly bizarre treatments, reading endless books and going on an all-out war to 'fix/cure' their child. Hope is high, reason is often out of the window, and relevant doctors, therapists and teacher's advice is heard and partially utilised, but not fully internalised as you believe that this is only a temporary 'hiccup'. This time is exceptionally draining on parents' emotional energy as well as their financial resources and can put the family unit at great risk on many levels

I spent a fortune on educational toys, turning Michael's room into a therapy room. I ruined Christmas and birthdays for him as he did not open fun presents, but yet more educational toys. I made my husband spend at least an hour with Michael at night in his 'therapy' room after he came home, exhausted from work. I kept promising my daughter Kim time alone with me, only to usually fall asleep on page two when reading her book in bed. I was in panic mode as I was repeatedly told that 'early intervention is essential' and I felt time was running out. It was a very exhausting and tense period for all.

As Kim was growing up, I became increasingly aware of how essential it was to balance my time and attention between her and my son with autism. What an endless and almost impossible task that was, often leaving me totally exhausted, guilt ridden, and with unhealthy tension in the home and in the marriage.

Michael came home from school with bite marks on two separate occasions and I asked that the school try to supervise him better, only to find out that his sister, Kim, had bitten him. It was most certainly not her fault but mine, as I knew that despite my best attempts and in my panic to 'fix' Michael, she had been neglected and was highly resentful. Additionally, something that was exceptionally difficult to get right were rules for both children and the consequences for breaking these rules! On several occasions when Kim did something wrong and I would tell her off, she would respond that 'Michael does it and does not get told off' and then I would to try to explain that 'he does not understand and that is why he does not get told off'. This was very difficult and frustrating for Kim.

I then found that – and I have seen this in many other parents of a child with autism – when Michael was about 8 years old, while still trying to do my best, there was a slight release of pressure and tension. I listened more to teachers and therapists, spent less time seeking out a 'cure' and started accepting that while the autism was a part of Michael that could not be removed, I could work hard to improve his outcomes. However, I feel that at this age, parents still do not fully internalise the possible lifelong implications of autism, which start sinking in when the child becomes a teenager. This was a very mixed time for me emotionally, as I took the intense pressure off myself, Michael and the family, but although I felt there could be further development, it was almost like a time of surrender and almost giving up hope.

It was also around the time Michael turned 12 that I had to accept that his next educational opportunity was at another school and he would have to be a weekly boarder. The phenomenal pain and anguish I went through as I started marking clothes and packing a large suitcase for him was horrific. I wanted to refuse this next step – I could not put my beautiful boy into boarding school, not see him every night, not bath him and have him at home in our family unit in the evenings. The tears poured, but apart from the fact that Michael needed this educational step, most importantly, my daughter Kim was finding it increasingly difficult to cope emotionally. Kim had stopped having friends to play at the house as she was embarrassed and nervous, she was withdrawing, and I knew for her sake, we needed to make this move.

The first night Michael was at boarding school, I was devastated and could not go near his room. Even though he went on Monday morning, came back Friday lunchtime and was home for the school holidays, it was heartbreaking. However, it did improve with time, and I saw Kim coming out of her shell and smiling a lot more.

After two years we realised that Michael's intellectual disability was too great for him to stay at Unica School. We persevered for a further year, but saw a dreadful decline in Michael's happiness and development. I cringe when I look back to that time. His specialist told me that I should take him out of the school as the pressure was too great for him. Michael clung to the home front door frame when we were taking him back, but as I could not face the fact that, at 15, this was the only education being offered to Michael, that his adulthood whether at home or in a centre had begun. So we pushed him and pushed him. I know hindsight is an accurate science, but I still hang my head in shame when I remember what I put my boy through.

By this stage, Kim had at least had a bit of a break, but it must have been hard for her to have Michael home again full time. Michael contracted the Coxsackie virus and therefore slept a lot and hardly moved around the house, which caused us great worry and sadness, but, as awful as it sounds, it did help with the readjustment to having Michael home full time. Kim was an absolute star, loving and caring for her brother while he was ill.

As Michael improved, our daily routine obviously became more difficult as his strength and activity levels increased. We kept going for a couple of months, with the old tensions and exhaustion growing again within the house, and Michael showing signs of boredom. A respite centre an hour away was recommended, which we duly contacted.

Shalom Respite Care Centre was designed for profoundly physically disabled residents, but the matron saw the sheer exhaustion on all our faces and agreed to take Michael. Again, the tears and separation anxiety welled up inside me.

When we took Michael to Shalom, my husband, daughter and an excellent friend and her daughters booked accommodation just down the road from the centre, in case Michael or the staff did not cope. Michael caused chaos for a couple of weeks, but the truly magnificent staff persevered, and Michael started to settle. I honestly believe in hindsight that Michael had a nervous breakdown and Shalom was a major part of his recovery. Michael is now a permanent resident at Shalom Respite Care Centre, and although it has not always been a smooth ride, he is very happy there and comes home every other weekend.

My husband Bob emigrated from the UK to South Africa in 1972 and I emigrated from the UK in 1979, so the bulk of our family is in the UK. So, while they have been of great support emotionally, we have never really had any physical family support here in South Africa. This is a hard and lonely situation to be in, but we have had supportive friends who have provided us with strength on many occasions.

Speaking of friends, over the years, we have obviously had many different circles of friends and sometimes I analyse which friends we do not see anymore and which friends, even after 30-odd years, are still very much part of our lives, even if we do not get to see them that often. I think that some of our friends we are no longer in contact with slowly weaned themselves away due to the difficulties we faced raising Michael. Either I was hardly present at the event I had organised in our home as I was chasing Michael around, or, if we were at their houses, I was chasing him to prevent damage to their property, still unable to avoid leaving a small trail of damage or mess when he had thrown a pot plant into their pool or spread his food across their tablecloth! There were definite categories of friends: those who would invite you round and when you said Michael was home and therefore you would be bringing him would say, 'Oh dear, let's make it another time', or those most appreciated friends who would say, 'Not a problem at all. It will be great to see him.' A child with autism soon sorts out your real friends! Over the years, we met many parents with a child with autism and often they were the best friends to socialise with – they were understanding and accepting of our son and their houses were autism friendly!

I also noticed that when we were with friends who were relaxed with Michael in their homes, we hardly even had any problems, but when we were at friends who did not really want Michael present, there were nearly always breakages or issues. Michael definitely picked up the vibe.

Another way I find myself differentiating between 'categories' of friends and family is that when I am with people or they phone, nearly all will ask about my daughter, but very few ask how Michael is. This is very hurtful and at times, depending on my mood and the person, I often say, 'Oh, and Michael is well too!'

The public's reactions to Michael when we are out also varies. There have been times when I have given an angry response to a look, comment or reaction from a member of the public, but there have been times too when I have come home and sobbed – it all depends on where my heart and mind are at that point.

I was once in a small food shop when Michael grabbed something out of a man's hands and put it back on the shelf. The man reacted rudely to Michael, at which point I jumped in, apologised and explained that Michael had autism and liked things in their right place, so please could the man put the packet in his basket or leave it on the shelf until I had taken Michael to the next aisle. The man (obviously well educated as he stood there in expensive clothes and shoes) then shouted at me that if my child had a problem, he should not be allowed out in public. In my fury, and with everyone in the shop standing still staring at the three of us, I pushed my trolley towards a staff member, asking her to please keep it safe for half an hour while I took my 'disgusting' child home. Tears pouring down my cheeks, I took Michael out of the shop and into the car to go home. On my return to the shop, my groceries had been tallied up, there was a bunch of flowers on the top and the shop assistant told me that after I left, everyone had glared at this man, so he had left the shop and the people had expressed their disgust in him and their sadness for me and Michael.

Another time, we had taken Michael to a restaurant and we were waiting for our food when an order for other people was placed on their table very close to ours, and Michael jumped up and grabbed a large handful of chips! That time, I took the blame and offered profuse apologies and new chips!

As Michael has an intellectual impairment as well as autism, his development to where he is now was very slow indeed. When he was about 7, I was in a bank queue with him and I had given him paper and a pen to keep him occupied. I then saw that for the first time he had drawn a circle – I jumped up and down with joy and praised him profusely, only to see the others in the queue looking very puzzled that I would show such joy with a child that age who had only drawn a scraggy circle! Anyway, the joy was mine and they could not take that away from me.

Slow development obviously brings a lot of frustration and heartache for parents, but at the same time I think the reaction to the achievements of a child with autism is often more emotional than the pride and job you feel at your 'normal' child's development.

When I reflect on some of the mistakes I made over the years trying to raise an autistic son, I do have to take into account that Michael was only diagnosed when he was 5, back in the dark ages of 1989, when hardly anyone knew about autism and there was a very limited range of appropriate intervention methods. This slightly relieves some guilt. Especially as before Michael was correctly diagnosed, I tried to raise him as a child with 'minimal brain dysfunction and speech delay' and therefore many of my methods aggravated situations and boosted all our frustrations. I think nowadays, with the much greater knowledge, while the path for parents is far from easy, it is so much more informed and supported.

I remember one day I was crying and Michael, aged about 6, walked up and laughed in my face. I was absolutely devastated and I screamed at him. Many years later, I read that people with autism often laugh at someone crying because they think your face is like a water pistol that you have previously taught them to play with and laugh at! I also remember getting so cross with Michael when he was young and how he used to laugh at me. Again, it is due to the fact that your face becomes distorted and red like the Punch and Judy show that used to make him laugh!

At the time, it was not funny, but I do have a chuckle every now and then when I remember that as Michael and I were walking along a pavement, an elderly woman ahead fell very badly, and Michael burst out into a very loud and intense laughter. I took him off at speed as others ran to this lady's aid – again, it was the type of situation that he laughed at when watching children's programmes and although I was shocked and quite horrified at the time, I now know why he reacted in that way!

Another thing that took us several years to work out, was that, as he got older, Michael less and less enjoyed going away on holiday. We thought we were great parents as we loaded Michael into the car with Kim to go to the seaside for two or three weeks. As Michael went from 5 to 8 years old, he became more withdrawn and started to make a lot of noise, which on the last holiday we took him on, we saw totally evaporate the minute we walked back through our home front door. Poor, poor Michael, as he has never spoken, he had no way to tell us and we did not really know at that point, just how much children with autism dislike change. The following year, with many tears and great sadness we went away and left Michael with a carer at home, where he was as happy as anything!

Kim has been a total rock throughout her teenage and adult years; she is totally dedicated to her brother and will do anything for him, and we are exceptionally proud of her and adore her for this. I do feel that however hard it was for us to send Michael to boarding school and then into residential care, this did save Kim, as well as her relationship with her brother.

My husband has been truly fantastic throughout. It is so much harder for men to accept that their only son will not be the one they dreamt of and that their home life is fraught with challenges, frustration and tensions. I am so lucky and privileged to have such a beautiful, strong and wonderful family.

Michael is now 32 years old and he is my beautiful six-foot 3-year-old! There are times that I am resentful that I still have to parent such a 'young child' – that I have had a 3-year-old for 29 years and my friends' children are married or independent and they do not have such a lifelong burden. I have times of desperately wishing Michael would 'just come right' and that this is all a bad dream. When I am in this bad place and I picture how Michael should be at 32 years, I feel very sad for him, but as I try to lift my soul, I realise just how much I would truly miss my autistic 3-year-old. I think of all the people I have met, the fantastic experiences I have had as a result of Michael, and my smile creeps back and I have a chuckle. I would never have had these experiences without him being autistic and, in a way, I should be grateful I have a son with autism whom I love with all my heart.

Chapter 7

JOAN AND JONATHAN

(AUSTRALIA)

'He ain't heavy – he's autistic'

Jonathan, our second son, was born in 1965 and diagnosed autistic before he was 3 years old. He was, and still is, non-verbal and ran the gamut of autistic behaviours during his childhood.

Since 1968, I have been involved not only with helping Jonathan, but also in developing programmes for autistic children generally, through the establishment of the Autistic Centre (now Mansfield Autism Statewide Services) and Mansfield Travelling Teachers (now Mansfield Autism Practitioners).

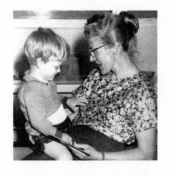

It is my firm belief that the best teaching environment for any child is real life, and with our own son we have tried to share with him all the normal experiences that the rest of the family enjoy. When he was 7 we travelled to England and South Africa, and this set the pattern. He is now an experienced and capable traveller, by plane, train, boat, bus and even cable car. He will go calmly into any house, sleep in any bed, and will tackle most meals. In 1984, we expanded his experience by taking him on a canoe safari in New South Wales, sleeping in a

tent and eating meals sitting on the ground. We repeated this enterprise in 1989 on the Daly River in the Northern Territory, sharing the river with fresh water crocodiles – by this time, Jonathan's paddling had improved considerably!

I introduced Jonathan to horse riding at the age of 5, riding bareback in front of me. During his teens and twenties, he rode a good deal, managing to trot and canter, but always on a leading rein. This came to an end when his trusty horse died, and we never found another one reliable enough to take her place.

We have a farm, which is an ideal venue for walks, camps and barbeques and has allowed Jon to take part in farm work. He has planted and watered trees, loaded and unloaded wood, spread out hay, and chopped out rushes and thistles. It sounds impressive, but he only works for short periods. His moment of glory came when he successfully pulled a calf – I had put the ropes on the feet but was not strong enough to deliver it. Jonathan grasped the rope, gave one heave, and the calf was out.

I opened the Mansfield Autistic Centre in 1978 as a residential school for autistic children, still the only one in Australia. This, of course, was for Jonathan's benefit, but incidentally has benefited a great many others. Much fundraising, lobbying and arguing with government departments was required to get this project going. Maintaining and developing it, often in the face of serious opposition, has been the pattern of my life until 2001, when I finally handed over the baton.

To balance his time in residential care, I try to give Jonathan at least one good holiday a year. He has camped and hiked in Kakadu, walked around Ayres Rock and Kings Canyon, and visited the Flinders Ranges and Cradle Mountain National Park. He has stayed on Brampton Island, Long Island, Fraser Island, Flinders Island and windswept Lord Howe Island, as well as in numerous holiday parks along the coasts of New South Wales and Victoria. Often, we have travelled as a family, but in recent times I have employed a staff member to assist me. Apart from being a relaxing break in routine, these trips have been valuable learning experiences for us both.

During the 1980s, we introduced a vocational training programme at the school, including such activities as gardening, lawn mowing, wood carving and making concrete garden ornaments. Jonathan particularly enjoys turning the cement mixer and has made this his personal responsibility.

Painting was introduced to the curriculum mainly for recreation, but gradually we discovered considerable talent in several of the students. We have held a number of successful exhibitions locally and one in Melbourne, which have led to regular and profitable sales. Our most successful artist has twice won a $1000 art prize, and Jonathan sells two to three pictures a year for prices between $100 and $300 – not counting some of his best work which I have hijacked to hang at home!

In 1988, two of the adults were able to move out from the junior residence into a home of their own (after about ten years of training for this!). I opened a separate adult unit to cater for Jonathan and three other young men. They have a residential supervisor and attend the day training centre from 9am to 4pm. It had been my intention to develop this programme to cater for people graduating from the junior school, but the government made it a condition of funding the adult residence that there should be no more enrolments!

During his twenties, Jonathan became depressed, his obsessional behaviour became worse, and he had episodes of inconsolable crying. He had a couple of admissions to a psychiatric unit in Melbourne and was started on a cocktail of antidepressants and antipsychotics.

Over a period of years, several different drugs have been tried with varying degrees of success. It can be difficult to judge if a drug is effective because Jonathan's behaviour patterns can fluctuate widely. For the past five years, he has settled well on a combination of Venlafaxine and Haloperidol. He shows no signs of depression but still has episodes of destructiveness (of property) and self-damage (cutting and picking his skin). His behaviour management programmes aim to occupy his time usefully and pleasantly, and to reduce opportunities for destructive behaviours. Jonathan is at his most relaxed when spending free time at the farm or on the beach.

What impact has Jonathan had on the rest of the family? Both my husband, Humphrey, and my elder son, David, have been a constant support not only with Jonathan, but the whole autistic enterprise. Despite a busy general practice, Humphrey has often joined us bush walking, swimming, canoeing and skiing at weekends with the children from the residence. All through his school and university years, David has been a vital part of our annual family camps. He was my right-hand man and very popular with the families and the young staff. He organised activities for the siblings, led walks, cooked barbeques and played a major role in the sports meeting and the concert. He certainly enjoyed himself and I believe he gained confidence and maturity.

As I write this chapter, Jonathan is 50 and I am 86, thus rapidly approaching my 'use-by date'. I no longer have the energy or physical strength to provide him with the activities he needs.

So, what have we achieved? Jonathan is living in supported accommodation which greatly exceeds the standards of Government Group Homes. He has excellent staff who are devoted to him and he comes home for one night every three weeks – when he frequently misbehaves! He is still non-verbal – which is restful – and  non-violent, which is fortunate as he is over six feet tall. He travels well and behaves well in restaurants, theatres and cinemas. His most useful skills are lawn mowing, concrete mixing, painting pictures and chopping vegetables. His worst behaviours are destructiveness, intermittent tearing up of clothing, furnishings and books, and self-damage such as cutting himself and pulling off skin and toe nails. He has also ground his teeth down to stumps by chewing on wood and metal, including chair legs and the edges of doors. All these activities are intermittent and appear to go in cycles.

So, have I really achieved very much with 47 years of hard work? How much has he benefited from a full and interesting life? Does he remember his adventures with pleasure? Does he have any clue that I love him?

I cannot answer these questions. All I can say is that he is safe, comfortable and well cared for, and around him has grown an organisation that has been of tremendous benefit to many other autistic people and their families.

Let that be our joint memorial!

Chapter 8

LIZ AND RICHARD

(ENGLAND)

When my son Richard was born on 12 February 1974, I thought he was the ugliest baby I had ever seen, but I adored him on sight. Not only did he look awful, he was awful. He cried incessantly, he never slept and he didn't suck.

So, how is it that I have ended up with this tall, handsome, independent man who is my son today, when one doctor told me that I would have to make up my mind that I would have to look after him for the rest of my life?

The road has been long and hard and fraught with difficulties, and only achieved with the help and support of family, friends and an excellent school.

It was apparent to me from the start that there was something wrong, but as Richard is also highly intelligent there were times when he would astound us all with some remark or act far beyond his years.

We did the rounds of paediatricians and child psychologists trying to find the answers, but to be frank, I think he perplexed them as much as he did us. Bearing in mind that this was the 1970s and not the Dark Ages, there were two things in particular that made things even more difficult than they might have been. First of all, it was impossible to get a diagnosis! I begged and pleaded for them to tell me what was wrong as I felt I needed to know what I was up against. The professionals that we saw refused to give us any clue as to the nature of his problems. All they would say was that they refused to put labels on people. This seems incomprehensible now, as we know that early diagnosis is of the utmost importance. What is worse is that they knew, as they recommended a school for autistic children, which gave us a clue.

The other great difficulty was the notion that the mother was to blame for causing the autism in her child. By the 1970s, this had been largely discredited, but it was apparent that many health care professionals still subscribed to this view. How on earth could anyone think that telling a mother she was to blame, even if it was true (which it isn't), could possibly help someone who was already suffering?

Of course, I knew nothing of this at the time and was often upset by the attitude of some of the professionals I went to for help, sometimes encountering unkindness and even hostility. On occasion, what sticks in my mind was when I was asked if he watched television. When I replied that he did not watch television, before I could expand on it and tell them that he didn't like the television as he preferred listening to the radio, this man said, 'Oh, of course you are the perfect mother.' I was so astounded that I couldn't say anything. I wouldn't stand for it now. I suppose if you are faced with this monster mother who you think has caused the whole thing, you wouldn't have much sympathy.

Unwittingly, I played right into their hands, being the type of person who always liked to be well dressed, with make-up and hair done, and if anyone came to the house, it would be clean and tidy with all the graffiti washed off the walls. How naive, how young I was.

Anyway, I must get on with telling you how the miracle of my son came about.

When Richard was just over a year old we went to live in Sweden. At that time, he had made no attempt to talk, he never seemed to eat or drink anything, although he must have as he survived. He was obsessed with water and regularly flooded the place out. If you stopped him getting to the taps he would have his head down the toilet. If there really was no water available, he would pour sand or if all else failed, it would be earth in the garden. This was the first of many obsessions, including wheels and cows.

Even now he still gets obsessions, which can be a difficulty. One in particular that sticks in my mind is when he became obsessed with having a title. It was triggered by when the government decided to try to reform the House of Lords. They got rid of some of the hereditary peers and announced that anyone could apply to become a peer. Richard sent off for all the relevant paperwork and filled it in and sent it off. Of course, he was refused, which I think was a big mistake on their part as if anyone could have shaken them up, it was Richard. At this time, my friend suggested that he could buy a title, as she said some friends of hers had done it and always got the best tables in restaurants and upgraded flights. So, that is just what he did. At first, he was adamant that everyone used his title so much so that even I used to get correspondence addressed to Lady Elizabeth, much to my delight. Like all his obsessions, this one seems to have run its course and he isn't nearly so insistent on everyone using the title now, although some organisations like the bank, for example, still use it.

Soon after we arrived in Sweden, we were invited to a lunch party, which led to a major breakthrough. An American man called me over to see Richard drinking his strong black coffee! After initially feeling aghast I began to think that perhaps he liked strong flavours, so the next day I ditched the milk and made him a cup of black coffee and he loved it. Also, I started to give him curry, spaghetti Bolognese and smoked salmon, which was a particular favourite. We have never looked back and to this day it is what he likes. The grandmothers disapproved.

After Sweden, we came home, briefly, and I had another son, much to Richard's disgust. Matthew, Richard's brother, couldn't have been more different. He was beautiful, he slept when he was supposed to, when he was awake he giggled and hardly ever cried, and he could suck. It was as if he knew that it was no good being difficult.

Matt was born at the end of October and after Christmas we went to live in Norway. Richard was almost 3 and still had made no attempt to talk. The airport in Norway was a NATO (North Atlantic Treaty Organisation) base and had anti-aircraft guns around the perimeter. When Richard saw this, he got very excited and lo and behold, said his first word, 'gun'. Soon afterwards we all went down with the most awful sore throats and none of us could speak at all, I was so afraid that it would put him off, but it didn't, and he hasn't stopped since!

While we were in Norway, Richard went to a very good preschool, which had recently opened and was run by Americans who understood him. They encouraged us to find a school in England for Richard when we returned. We were so fortunate in that Linden Bridge is now world-renowned and I believe has a waiting list, but in those days, he was able to get in straightaway.

This led to another breakthrough for me, if not for him. Having been completely isolated, I met other parents and children with similar, although not the same, problems and it was a revelation.

Once Richard was settled in school, we had a few years of relative calm until 1985, when his father was killed in a car crash in Iraq. Surprisingly, instead of having a negative effect, this seemed to galvanise both my sons into action. Matthew shot up from being in the middle of his class (which I was very satisfied with) to top of the class, and walked off with all the prizes. Richard's headmistress met me at the door of the school on parents' evening to tell me how well he was doing and how pleased they were with him. I am not sure whether this was because they were getting a bit of extra attention because of the tragedy, but whatever the reason, it had a good effect.

At around this time, a very good friend who was a retired teacher asked me if she could take Richard on as a challenge to help him with reading and writing. She did this, first once a week and then twice a week for years for an hour after school. He joined the Cubs and then the Scouts and went swimming and camping with them. He went on holidays with the school and began boarding for two nights a week.

At some time, although I cannot remember exactly when it was, I had a eureka moment. I think it came about because I was so consumed with worry that suddenly I couldn't take any more. I had always been looking for a cure, which seems ridiculous now, but I was searching for a magic pill or a piece of the puzzle that could be slotted in and everything would be alright. In this moment, I realised that there was no cure or magic potion and it was okay. Richard was as he was and I had to accept it.

The worry at that time was moving on and we had to think about what was to happen when he left school. In any event, he went to a residential college, which he says he hated every minute of. He came home every other weekend and for the holidays and whether he hated it or not, it did help him to become more independent. After a while he had to do his own shopping, cooking and washing. He was there for three years and when he turned 19 he started to learn to drive, driving being his latest obsession at the time.

When he left the residential college, I didn't know what to do with him, but it was recommended that he went to a local college, which was an unmitigated disaster. He was plunged into the mainstream, which he was unprepared for and was subjected to bullying from students and staff alike. It was so bad that his social worker was prompted to write a letter of complaint.

I forgot to mention that his school had offered him a job doing gardening and caretaking for one morning a week and by this time, he had passed his driving test. It took him a long time, but he eventually succeeded with the help of a driving instructor with expertise in teaching people with disabilities.

The experience at the local college had dented his confidence and although we tried many other avenues, nothing ever worked out.

Some time before all this, I had joined a local pressure group with other parents to try to get the local council to provide accommodation for people like Richard. After a few years, I had to leave because I got a job, but later I was able to go back again. I was horrified, but not surprised, to hear that no progress whatsoever had been made in my absence. Then, after more years, suddenly the council agreed to build the perfect place. This, again, took some time and unfortunately by the time it was finished, Richard had managed to alienate everyone involved, so it was decided that it would be inappropriate for him to move in. This was disappointing, but apparently the process had involved him being on the council housing list and although it seemed pointless, we decided that he should remain on the list.

After yet more years, I had a call from the council to say that Richard had reached the top of the list and they had a flat available for him. We were so amazed that our first reaction was to refuse. We were completely unprepared, but decided the least we could do was to go and look at it. It was perfect; we couldn't refuse it. It was a lovely one-bedroom flat in well-kept grounds and about a mile away from me. Richard has been living independently (with support) for about 20 years, and he manages very well. He doesn't live as I would like him to live because I wish that his flat was cleaner and tidier and that he didn't hoard so much. When he was younger, I could go in and clean the place and tidy up but now he doesn't like me to do it. I can understand that he doesn't want his mother poking around his things and I have asked for help for him from social services on several occasions. The person who comes to assess the situation always agrees that he needs help and says that they will recommend that he should get it, but then a few weeks' later we get an apologetic letter saying although they have recommended that Richard should get this, the manager has vetoed it.

He is much better with computers than I am and is a real carer. For years, he cared for an elderly man in his block of flats until he died. Now he has transferred to a younger man in the block who has multiple sclerosis. I don't think he likes this to be generally known as it doesn't go with the 'hard man' image he likes to project.

He has been in *The Undateables* on Channel 4 and became quite famous, and, before you ask, he still doesn't have a girlfriend. Now I have more or less reached the stage that we are at now and I have read through what I have written, I feel it is gloomier than I thought it was going to be and I haven't even mentioned being accused of benefit fraud! I wanted it to be more lighthearted and amusing but, although I am sure there will be many more challenges ahead, I think the message is to never give up and to always live in hope.

It still isn't easy, but at least, and at long last, Richard got a formal diagnosis when he was in his early twenties, prompted by

an unhelpful person in social services who decided he wasn't autistic at all. He was diagnosed by Dr Attard, then a leading expert on autism in the county.

In conclusion, I must tell you that genetically I come from a family of autistic people. They are all perfectly able to function, but have a reputation for eccentricity. I even have that reputation myself and I can't think why, so perhaps it is all my fault after all, just not in quite the way those doctors all those years ago meant.

Chapter 9

MARY AND KOKELETSO

(SOUTH AFRICA)

Kokeletso (Koki) was born on 24 February 1984. In his first couple of years, although not a particularly easy period as Koki was very active, we felt that his development was on track. It was, as for many parents I gather, only when he went to nursery school, that his teacher and we as parents noticed that Koki was not really like the other children. He had speech, but there was often a delay in his responses, such as when singing nursery rhythms. Additionally, his method of play was different, as was his interaction with the other children at school.

It was when Koki was aged between 6 and 7 and he was enrolled in school that, again, we were told that he really was not coping with formal education and that he was 'different'. We then took him to Ga-Rankuwa Hospital, now known as Dr George Mukhari, where he was seen by a psychiatrist who, on observing his behaviour, decided he had attention deficit hyperactivity disorder (ADHD) and put him on Ritalin.

Back home we went, but the school still did not manage to cope with Koki in the classroom, so they recommended that he be moved to a special class at another primary school. This path led to another dead end, as this school refused to accept him, as did other special schools, some saying he was too 'high functioning' and others saying he did not fit their criteria.

Koki hated school and it was so hard for us to keep trying to get him into a school that he would enjoy and benefit from. The poor boy went to several different schools, none with great success until he ended up at Coronation Training Centre from 16 to 21 years old. During this traumatic time and observing Koki from a different perspective, I became increasingly aware that he spent a lot of time alone, happily playing, not particularly with toys, but rather with a small stick or leaf. It puzzled me, but he seemed happy and chatted away to himself. Though saying that, there were times when Koki would suddenly start crying for no apparent reason and this disturbed us a great deal. The other aspect that increasingly became apparent to us was that Koki, though speaking, was not truly communicating in an appropriate way.

Embarrassment was common in our daily lives, as Koki said it as he believed and felt it! If you were fat, he would tell you; if you were smelly, he would tell you! Koki's brothers and sisters did not like being in his company and the feeling was mutual! Koki used to go and find people who were nice to him and when I asked him why he did not want to be at home with his siblings he said, 'They do not like me, so why should I play with them?'

My husband, Kenneth, while watching Koki evolve in front of us, with his 'inappropriate' behaviours and the situations we could find ourselves in thanks to Koki, would smile and tell me and others not to get upset, that we must all accept Koki as our God-gifted child. Kenneth's gentleness and acceptance helped me a great deal, but Koki was not fully accepted by our friends and relatives. We found ourselves being shunned and often excluded from family gatherings, which, obviously, we found very hurtful. Not knowing what was actually wrong with Koki, we found it difficult to defend his behaviours and had to deal with the ever-prevalent suggestion that we take him to a traditional healer to be cured. Sometimes friends or relatives suggested an African remedy and to appease them, as long it was not dangerous in any way, I would try their suggestions. There were many tense times at gatherings when Koki would not like the way people spoke to him, or about him, in front of him and he would let them know what he thought!

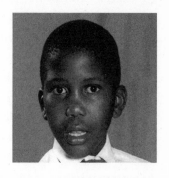

When Koki was 10 years old, we were at his grandmother's house for a family gathering for the unveiling of a tombstone. Koki was pacing around, in and out of the house and his aunt told him to settle down and stop getting in everyone's way, to which he replied, 'You cannot tell me what to do. This is not your house, it is my grandmother's house!'

Koki had his way of understanding things. Because his father is quite plump, he told a bus driver who he felt was troubling him that if the driver saw his father he would not continue to do what he was doing, because he would get a clear message as to what would happen to him. When Koki's father fetched him from the bus one day, the driver laughed so much that Kenneth had to ask him what was the matter. The driver told him the story. But, when Kenneth one day said to Koki, 'You know that I am very strong?' Koki said, 'No, that is just fat.'

Another incident that still makes me smile is when a person asked Koki to go to the liquor store to buy beer for him. Koki immediately said, 'No, I am not 18 yet and therefore cannot go there.' Additionally, Koki has an outstanding memory and on many occasions we would be dumbfounded when he would remember something small from his childhood, and this would be brought into the context of the present time. While impressed with these recollections, we were painfully aware of how much greater Koki's expressive communication was as opposed to his receptive communication. We had to be very careful and double check that Koki had fully understood what we had said to him. There were many occasions when we felt that Koki had heard and internalised what we had said, but, in actual fact, he really had not fully understood why we had said it.

When Koki asked us a question and we thought we had answered well, he could repeat the question several times over and this was when we realised that in fact he had not understood or processed our answer.

As parents, we were criticised because we would allow Koki to keep repeating questions and we would adapt our home, routine and reactions to manage Koki's behaviours – we adapted our life to him. We were told his behaviours were because he was spoilt and because of the way we did things to suit him. To a degree, we understood people's reactions and comments to Koki, as truthfully, the knowledge on autism was very poor, especially among the African communities, so that is why Koki was labelled as 'naughty', 'badly brought up' and 'rude'.

Over the years, Kenneth has expressed his disappointment that fathers really do not get that involved with their special needs children and therefore he often felt alone and judged by other male friends and family members.

One day I was sitting at home with Koki when I came across

an article in a magazine which referred to a condition called 'autism'. Because of my work as a domestic worker, I once worked for a family that had a 6-year-old boy who had autism. But, my understanding of the condition was minimal, and I don't even think the parents had a full understanding of the condition. That is why even when I saw the same signs that the little boy had displayed, I kept saying to myself: but my son speaks, this cannot be autism. He spoke well and all the children I had come across that were diagnosed with autism could not speak and were not nearly as 'capable' as my son. After some thought and rather through desperation, I decided I should phone the National Director of Autism South Africa (ASA), who had written the article. Jill Stacey was not at the office that day, but she phoned me back the next day and opened my eyes to the fact that there is a great range in the manifestations of autism and that the fact that Koki had good speech did not mean that he was not autistic. Jill referred me to a specialised psychiatrist for an assessment, which, at Koki's age of 23, eventually gave us the right answer – he was on the autism spectrum. Dr Benn put Koki on medication for his high levels of anxiety, as he noted that Koki appeared to have petit mal epilepsy. Koki never had a fit, but he did have periods of seeming to be absent from us. Yet, after all these years and now with the correct diagnosis, there were still no answers for us as to what we could do to further help Koki.

At this time, I started attending an ASA parent support group and spending time at its offices, getting to know more about autism and how I could help other parents like myself. I noticed how the parents just wanted a quick fix and medication as a cure, because in many cases they had not had a reasonable explanation of what autism is, and hadn't been told that if the child is put on certain medication, that medication is not to cure the condition. There are also minimal resources available for parents, especially for the more peri-urban and rural African parents with minimal income. Parents came and went too fast to the support group meetings and therefore went home despondent, as there were minimal special need schools in their area, and the staff in those had never heard of autism and thus were not keen to put a child with autism on their long waiting list.

I was thrilled in 2008 to be employed by Autism South Africa as the Regional Development Officer for Limpopo (a rural province in South Africa), the post which I still hold today.

From day one, I have done my utmost to lobby provincial government departments to offer training in autism to their teachers, social workers and other relevant professionals. I instigated support groups in differing areas and I encouraged people to come and speak to the parents to increase their understanding of autism. I worked with grandparents and other family members to enhance their understanding and acceptance of autism. Tribal leaders were high on my list in a tactful attempt to explain the physiology of autism and try to dispel myths that these children are a punishment from God for the sin of a forefather, or that they are possessed by the devil and need bleach poured down their throat to make them vomit out the devil. I saw children tied to beds, locked in a backroom as the parents did not want their neighbours to see their 'punishment from God' and ask what dreadful sin their forefathers had committed.

It has been a long, hard path with many obstacles, but I have made definite inroads and there are many more classes with autism-trained teachers in this province, the provincial government is making provisions for our children, there are better assessment services and more parents and their extended families are understanding and working well with their autistic family member.

During this time, as I was reaching out to assist others, Koki was doing his utmost to achieve vocational skills for his future. He attended a vocational therapy unit, which he enjoyed, but his main passion was to become a policeman.

Koki joined the police reservists as he so wanted to fight crime! Sadly, the policemen did not really make a great amount of effort to understand and accommodate him. Koki applied to Johannesburg Central Police station for training, which he underwent, but even after this, he was not accepted to become  a police reservist. Koki remains as a volunteer for a local neighbourhood watch group and he is determined that he will keep on applying to become part of the police force.

At the time of writing, Koki has joined me at the offices of Autism South Africa. He comes to work with me three days a week where, with the assistance of visual schedules, he collates material for training courses, monitors stock, ensures adequate material levels, as well as checking that staff and visitors are regularly provided with tea and coffee! Koki now also wants to learn to work on a computer and he would like to focus on the area of logistics. It is wonderful when parents visit the offices of Autism South Africa as they are most impressed with what Koki has achieved and how productive and fulfilled he is when undertaking his tasks.

Koki is now 33; he has laid many challenges at our feet, with many more to come, I expect, but he has enriched our lives. Despite negative statements being made regarding his prognosis and behaviours, we are still excited about his ongoing learning and development, as well as the joy he brings to us each and every year.

Chapter 10

MERRY AND NEERAJ

(INDIA)

'Rajat,' said Priti to her 5-year-old, 'please get me the book from my bedside table. And then get Aunty Merry a glass of water.' I was visiting my sister-in-law who was putting her feet up after finishing various chores. How lucky, I thought, to be able to do this! Oh, yes, I know, children are not born to serve their parents. But, how lovely when they do! Neeraj, my son, did not even look at me when I called. Or do anything I asked him to! Rather, I spent the entire day trying to redo, re-stick, and repair everything that he had – with great abandon – undone, unstuck, and broken at home.

A couple of years after this wishful thinking, Neeraj got his diagnosis of autism. Now, many years later, he happily fetches and carries and does chores that I set him. And much more. So, wishes do come true!

But in between, life with Neeraj has been a rollercoaster ride.

Before Neeraj was born, I had a career. After he came I opted to put it on hold for a couple of years. I wanted to enjoy my time with my little one until he was 2 or 3. Maybe until he started nursery school, I thought. But, watching my son at 2, I knew I had to give him more time. I will wait, I thought, until he is 5 before getting back to work.

And then bam! Autism happened.

We discovered this fellow traveller called autism and learned that this was the reason Neeraj did, and did not do, various things.

It started me on a journey to understand autism as much as to understand Neeraj and myself.

Before autism came into the picture, I was viewed as just the typical lousy mum. I had a close 'friend' who was persuaded that Neeraj's 'bad behaviour' was purely an outcome of my poor parenting. I was clearly an over-indulgent mother. If only I was strict with him, all would be well. She was not alone. There were friends, extended family, paediatricians, strangers, shopkeepers, in fact a large part of the discovered world, who all had an opinion on my parenting skills.

And then came autism, reinforcing those beliefs. I did not spend enough time with Neeraj. I was not warm. I spoke to him as if he was a grown-up, no wonder he was the way he was. I did not discipline him enough. I did not love him enough. Plus, everyone now also had an opinion on how to make Neeraj 'alright'. Somebody's neighbour's uncle was a doctor who had fixed somebody's child of a similar 'malady'. Somebody's aunt's second cousin knew a holy man whose potions had the power to make one 'well'. The neighbour's son's boss's family knew of a shrine where no prayer went unanswered. On trains, in the park, at the optician's, waiting in a random queue, people thought nothing of buttonholing me after observing us for five minutes, and launching into advice on something to 'fix' the squirming child accompanying me.

Neeraj, of course, did everything he could to ensure I maintained my dubious reputation. He was a gorgeous little boy who did his own thing. A charged particle, perpetually in motion, he checked, spat out, explored, took apart, dropped, smeared, threw out, and contemplated in bubble-wrapped repetitiveness. Or he tested his vocal chords, which had a surprising power of their own. In the early years, Neeraj did not speak and when he did, he did barely. But he more than made up for it with the volume and intensity of his vocalisations.

When we were handed the diagnosis of autism, it was akin to being picked up by the scruff of the neck and dropped into a very deep and very dark and empty pit. We were handed the diagnosis and perfunctorily shoved into an information vacuum. There was no information on what I could do, no reference to professionals who could help and who I could consult with, no organisation or institution that could support me in helping Neeraj. Every way I turned, I ended up bumping into a wall.

Those were the dark ages of information: pre-internet, pre-Jessica Kingsley Publishers, pre-social media! When the psychiatrist who diagnosed Neeraj sent me out into the big bad world, Google was yet to come into existence. The internet was still to knock on India's doors. Except for the doctor who made the diagnosis, no one seemed to know or to have heard of autism. On learning of Neeraj's diagnosis, I would be asked, 'what is that?' It felt strange that my son had something that had changed our lives forever and I didn't know what that was, seemed to have no way of knowing, and could not explain to people what it was when they asked me. I would parrot the doctor's words about 'communication and social impairment'. No big deal, people would say. 'My nephew spoke late and look at him now. Don't worry.' 'Mrs Khan's son is so brilliant, and he is so shy and reclusive. Don't worry.'

I was not worried, I was lost. Watching my son, I knew people were making incorrect assumptions but I could not put my finger on why. I just knew. We seemed to be speaking different languages: me versus everyone else. I felt very alone. I was dismissed as a fussy mother, and my bafflement was de-legitimised. It was a strangely disenfranchising feeling.

Years later when I began to finally 'get' autism, I also started gaining an insight into the sense of helplessness that those with autism must live with – of having experiences, thoughts and emotions, but not the words with which to express and communicate those within a world that seems to view and understand things from a completely different perspective. And just as I had wished all those years ago that people would not make assumptions about what the diagnosis meant for Neeraj and me, I know now that Neeraj and others like him must certainly want us to not make assumptions about what living with autism means for them.

Someone eventually directed me to a special needs school. Seeking help, I tracked down the school in a converted home within a quiet residential area of Calcutta. Entering the place, I found myself in a small central room, which had doors leading off to many other rooms. In the middle of the central concourse sat a wooden chair with a flat piece of wood locked across the two arms of the chair and holding in a boy of around 9. Plump and lost, he sat there seemingly unaware of the movement around him, a contemplative island in the centre of the bustle around him; a life form carved in enforced immobility to be commented on, observed and exclaimed over.

So, this was autism!

I recalled my son in a similar chair at 18 months. At that age, food and Neeraj were identical poles on two magnets, frantically repelling each other with determined force. I despaired of being able to have him and his mouth stay still anywhere near food. I finally acquired a highchair, firmly believing it would help him learn to stay in place for his meals. It is pretty clear that the highchair was designed by a clenched-jawed, harassed, and determined parent to be a feeding prison. You trap and immobilise the little human into a contraption that is 30 inches off the ground. Having got the head and mouth into position, you spoon in the mash from the bowl into the unresisting mouth. In 20 minutes the job is done, and you wipe and release the child. But, clearly that parent had not accounted for Neeraj. Placed into his highchair with the tray across the front, it would take him barely 20 seconds before he was up and free and climbing over the arm. After struggling for a few days trying to get him to stay in the chair and get food between his reluctant lips, terrified that if I turned my back he would speedily fall and crack his skull, I decided to junk the chair. Clearly a chair was not created that could keep him in place.

Before the diagnosis, I had believed I was messing up. I thought that this is what childhood was all about and as Neeraj got older, things would get better. This was just an extended phase of the terrible twos that had inexplicably extended into the threes and beyond. But it would of course come to an end. I just had to learn the right way of child rearing. Once I did, then we would not be reeling from catastrophe to catastrophe, as we seemed to be doing.

The diagnosis, when it came, unravelled my beliefs. Yes, it was not my fault. But hey, the crazy churn of our lives was not a passing phase either! This was for keeps. This was not going anywhere. This was to be our life – for life!

That was what had led me to the little boy in the chair.

Over the next few years Neeraj made his way through several schools with varying results. And I made my way through the only book I could find – Lorna Wing's *Autistic Children: A Guide for Parents*, and a few journals – *Communication* magazine from the National Autistic Society, *Autism Advocate* from the Autism Society of America – that I managed to source despite snail mail and fixed-line phones. Together, we bumbled through life doing some things right and getting a great many things woefully out of whack.

Through all this, Neeraj had his phases – passing phases, sometimes very long in the passing, and laced with very strong obsessions and impulses while they lasted. Still barely verbal, Neeraj had learned to climb over the parapet of the balcony outside the living room and, holding on precariously to the railing, walk on the narrow four-inch ledge over a one-storey drop. Heart in mouth, I realised that the more I tried to stop him, the more he got obsessed with the activity. Perhaps if I let him be, he would give it up.

Soon the walk on the ledge had an entertaining conclusion for Neeraj. He would walk the ledge to the end of the parapet, turn the corner, clamber down onto the balcony over the driveway half a floor down, and enter the studio apartment it was attached to! The young woman residing in the apartment would offer Neeraj a cola, which he would drink, and then come up the stairs and back home.

Another was a phase where he was fascinated with head gear. Anything on our heads, other than our naturally growing thatch, was a matter of fascination. Anything on our heads other than our own hair had to come off. Scarf, sunhat, hairband, cap, dark glasses, anything I propped on my head was immediately removed.

Out for a walk one day, we were enjoying the lovely post-winter Delhi sun inside the quite residential 'colony' that we lived in. We passed the occasional pedestrian. Coming towards us from the opposite direction was a youngish man. As he neared us, I had barely noticed his expensive, well-tailored clothes before Neeraj's arm swung upwards. Before I knew what was happening the man was minus what I now realised was a toupee on his head. The former was now lodged in the dry three-feet-deep ditch on the side of the road. Everything happened so fast that I did not have the time to react.

As I was apologising to the now semi-hairless and speechless with surprise young man, and wondering how to engineer the jump into the ditch, much to my relief I spotted a teenager sauntering our way. I begged him to jump in and retrieve the toupee, which I then ceremoniously handed over to the rightful owner.

My apology for the behaviour of my 10-year-old hooligan was not considered abject enough. The man's expression clearly indicated that I was an unfit mother, but I did not want to yell at Neeraj and turn the whole situation into an interesting experience for him. Besides, although I was mortified, I was also tickled and surprised at the power of observation Neeraj had just demonstrated; I was in awe! That was an expensive and well-fitted toupee. When perched on the man's head, there was no way one could tell that it was not growing out of his scalp. Yet Neeraj could!

It was many years later that I learned about central coherence and the power of detailed thinking that our children on the spectrum are blessed with. At that time, I could only marvel in ignorance.

Another headgear-related experience was far more drastic. Heading down the stairs one day we turned the corner to encounter a turbaned young man coming up, the turban urgently crying out to Neeraj, 'Look, I am headgear!' Neeraj's hand swooped and had barely brushed the turban when the young man's arm went up with double the speed and landed a sharp thwack on the side of Neeraj's face.

As he was a Sikh gentleman, the turban was connected to his faith and he was not going to put up with any monkey business.

With the passage of time, our life continued to get more and more difficult. Despite several special needs schools he attended, Neeraj only seemed to get more and more challenging. His school notebook was a litany of spectacles thrown, other children hit, cups thrown a floor down, clothes soiled, books ripped, and the retributory deprivation of his 'tiffin' that followed. Under the pretence of the normality of our lives, a kind of sheer desperation slowly crept in.

Seeking answers, I explored schools in the UK and the USA, and finally managed to get myself some training in America. It was very short yet intense and fascinating training.

Back in India, armed with an army of mini audio cassettes of our training sessions and a notebook full of assiduously scribbled notes to fall back on, I set up a home programme with Neeraj. Locked up monk-like in our apartment, we kept at it for a year and a half. It was hard work, and loads of fun. It was in those 18 months that I really discovered Neeraj and got to know the person he was. And I began to enjoy him. After Neeraj's diagnosis I had found one book in the British Council Library that carried a paragraph on autism and referred to 'refrigerator mothers' that had bolstered all the judgements on my parenting. All these years later I now stopped agonising over my role in Neeraj's autism. For the first time in a small way, I also began to understand autism beyond the theoretical explanations that I had learned to spew.

When we decided to come out of our self-imposed exile, parents who I had known for some years came to visit and were surprised by the changes in Neeraj. Now they wanted me to help them help their children. Somewhere, while trying to help them find answers, I started a movement that became known as Action For Autism.

Neeraj was now doing well and seemed to be over the most challenging phase. Of course, he still had occasional meltdowns, and so did I! Neeraj had what is often referred to as Kanner autism. He was also one of those who just did not seem to learn through imitation. Everything had to be taught with a high level of prompting. In addition, there were significant challenges with motor co-ordination. His verbal communication had grown but was still limited to basic needs. All other verbalisations were in response to clear and specific questions. Any spontaneous communication was like a direct blessing from above. In the car one day, Neeraj suddenly said, 'Girl riding a bicycle.' Surprised, I looked at him and asked, 'What?' He looked ahead and repeated, 'Girl riding a bicycle.' And there, indeed, was a girl up ahead riding a bicycle. Neeraj had never made such a declarative observation before, sharing his interest in something that he had noticed. Having made the observation, he sat gazing out of the window Buddha-like while I convulsed with joy and excitement beside him.

Another day out at a cafe, we had ordered some snacks and juice. The juice arrived in tall glasses full of ice, a very new experience for him. He sat there observing my friend's daughter reach for a drinking straw, push it in her drink through the ice, bend the straw at the 'elbow' and take a sip. He too reached for a straw, lodged it in the ice in his glass, bent the straw towards himself and sipped. He started imitating late, but whenever he did, it felt like a party.

Social ostracising is one of the most devastating experiences for most people on the spectrum. One of my aims for Neeraj, despite the severity of his condition, has been that he learns whatever will make negotiating the social world a little less challenging. When he had just turned 18, at a New Year's Eve party at a friend's home, Neeraj stood around looking dapper with a drink of cola in hand, occasionally taking a bite of an hors d'oeuvre that uniformed waiters were taking around. Then the music started up. I slow danced with him and the piece had barely come to a stop when, to my surprise, a young girl came up and asked him for a dance! Watching the two on the floor, as she tried to chat him up, I saw the realisation dawn on her face that he was different. What was wonderful was that it did not diminish her pleasure in dancing with him, matching him step for awkward step.

But soon after, for reasons too complex and personal to explain, Neeraj suddenly spiralled through a phase of anxiety, depression, and I know not what else. It manifested in behaviours that were extremely complex and challenging, leading to situations that often verged on the unsafe. He needed to hit. And since my body was invariably and conveniently present whenever he had a meltdown, I had to learn to be focused and light on my feet. At home I learned to skip out of reach, though not always successfully, and Neeraj learned to clasp his hands or hit his sturdy teakwood bed to help bring down his tension. Each day, he would have eight or ten sessions of hitting the bed along with heart-thumpingly loud shouting, which would last up to 20 or 30 minutes till he felt under control. After a few months, the bed was no longer in one piece!

At the height of this agonising phase, Neeraj did not leave home for over six months except for brief outings. On one of these outings, I optimistically took him for a walk in the neighbourhood park. We started out happily singing 'Strawberry Fields Forever', when suddenly, his mood changed, his face darkened, and before I could strike a Mohammad Ali position of defence I got a massive whack on my side and fell on the grass.

One thing I knew was to never let a crowd collect. For instead of helping him calm down, it just escalated his distress and anger. Having landed a punch, Neeraj's tension diminished marginally. Before there could be a recurrence, I quickly picked myself up along with the sharp pain in my side and we trotted back home. I found later that I had cracked a rib. That was the first of a few more rib-cracking experiences!

When stressed, Neeraj's hands needed to connect hard with something that would give satisfying resistance. That is why hitting the bed worked. When the bed was not in the vicinity it would be the closest human – or a wall, a door, a mirror, a table, just about anything resistive. The home we lived in at that time resembled a war zone. Frames without mirrors, doors coming off their hinges, door frames coming off the wall, glass tops missing from tables, plaster coming off walls.

Interestingly, Neeraj never hit our resident dog!

The number of unknown pedestrians Neeraj has walloped would be in a very comfortable two digits. That is in addition to all the known people who have been the subject of his ministrations. A person could be walking down the street minding his own business a little ahead of Neeraj, who would unexpectedly enter a dark mood. Suddenly, he would dart like a bolt of lightning and his hand would connect swiftly and heavily with the man's back.

As they lurched after being punched, most people were completely taken aback and at a loss as they stared angrily at the huge young man looking at them with an expression of part anger and part contemplation. Fortunately, on all those occasions, no one called the police, which makes me believe that despite discrimination and stigma, in India we are somewhat accommodating of unusual behaviours.

Driving was necessary, but fraught with unexpected developments. A six-foot-two mass of tension in the car resulted in damaged dashboards and seats, the danger of a crash, and frequently interrupted rides to help Neeraj bring his tension down before I could resume driving. In time, we hired a driver. With both of us now in the back seat, my job was to protect the driver – who was placed enticingly in front of Neeraj's out-of-control hands – as well as to keep myself in one piece. I became an expert at blocking at the speed of light and, when necessary, at curling my head down so that the sturdiest part of my body – my back – could take the brunt of Neeraj's attention.

This phase lasted many years. The intensity lessened, as did the frequency, and it took its time to slowly fade. While it lasted, and for a long time after, it was like living with a caged tiger! Neeraj's moods could not be predicted; at least, I did not have the skills to do so. Since I could not anticipate when he might have another episode, I had to learn to be a smart responder. I developed laser sharp focus, and strategies that no manual on autism could ever teach me.

Some of the triggers that brought about Neeraj's breakdown have not gone away completely. What has changed is his ability to regulate his emotions and keep a hold on how he expresses them.

Neeraj works at Aadhaar, the sheltered workplace we have set up at Action For Autism. He is independent in many ways, and needs support in many others. The wonderful thing is that he has learned to be happy. And he knows his opinion matters. He still does lose it sometimes. But there is maturity in our parent–child relationship.

There is another level of maturity that Neeraj has shown in recent years. Six years ago, I brought my 90-year-old father to live with us. My father and Neeraj had to share a room. Rather, Neeraj had to share his room with my father. Used to having a room to himself, Neeraj accommodated his Dadu cheerfully. He would fetch, carry, and do whatever Dadu asked without complaint. Both went to work together at Aadhaar where my father, at 90, came to be the senior most colleague.

About a year ago, after a second fall and second hip surgery, my father's behaviour started undergoing a change. He had delusions and held loud conversations with imaginary people in the middle of the night. He would get Neeraj up and ask him questions to which the poor chap did not have the answer or the words to respond with. After incontinence accidents, my father would be angrily certain that someone had poured water over his bedclothes. Advancing age, dementia and Alzheimer's coupled with his frustration at his slowing physical and mental faculties. I would tell Neeraj that Dadu was very old and this is what people do when they get old, that he was like a little child, and we could help Dadu feel better. Amazingly, Neeraj did not get angry or frustrated with his Dadu. Instead, he would cheerfully do my father's bidding, helping him on with his socks or shirt, fetching him the newspaper or some water. When not sure of Dadu's confused demands, Neeraj would rock and gaze into his face with a gentle smile.

The temptation is to pat myself on the back and believe that I have taught my son so much! Yes, I have. Like every mother, I have struggled each day to help tweeze out little drips and drops of skills that could turn into a flow, to cheer each effort that would make Neeraj's life easier and, by extension, mine. I have helped him over and over and over again in squeezing the tube of paste, making his bed, laying the table, counting out change, locking the door, keeping his footwear in their rightful places, buttering his toast, saying hello, towelling him, staying happy, walking safely down the road. I have expressed my love in concrete and simple ways so that he could learn from me. And I have wept and exulted the day my boy-turning-into-a-man said, 'Love Mama' for the first time.

Some children need a wee bit of teaching. Some need large gobs of it. But we all have to teach our children. That is what parenthood is about. But few children teach their parents life lessons on acceptance, patience, sensitivity, about being non-judgemental, and being a better person. Parenting is a tough job. Parenting a child with autism comes with its own challenges. Parenting Neeraj has been particularly adventuresome. However, from Neeraj I learned that while being mum to him has been a lot of work, being Neeraj has been tough at a level that I can never, ever gauge. If living with a person with autism is tough, living with autism is way more complex and challenging in a world that is not really ready to understand and is mostly unforgiving of people who do not fit the mould.

All of us who live with loved ones with autism want the world to be understanding and accepting of their oddities and quirks.

We are dismayed and upset when people stare, or show annoyance of their flapping, running and squealing. Yet we ourselves are quick

to annoyance and embarrassment when our children indulge in perseverative behaviours, when they run, touch, screech, pull, explore. If we have so much difficulty in accepting our own children, how can we expect the world to be any different? Neeraj has taught me the beauty of leading by example. If I want to change the world, I have to accept him for the person he is – stims, mood swings, sudden eruptions and all.

Neeraj makes me want to help him be the best he can be. He has made me his ally and the ally of others like him. And in doing so he has been the catalyst for the autism movement in India.

Much has changed in all these years. Of course, the judgemental eyes are still there. As long as there are people there will be blame and censure. But, I have learned to do the best I can and leave others to their opinions.

Like every mother, I hope Neeraj will have a good life after I am gone. We do not have any state systems for that in India. Action For Autism has stepped up to set up a group home that I hope will lead to others. In the meantime, we try to do the best we can. We work at acceptance, happiness, serenity. Yes, it's work, but satisfying work. Whenever Neeraj bumps into me during the course of the day, or when he meets me at the end of the day, his goofy grin and the absolute pleasure that lights up his eyes make my life so worth everything – far more than all the chores he now uncomplainingly does.

Chapter 11

PETRA AND MICHAEL

(NAMIBIA)

Refrigerator mothers? No! Rather: investigative forensic journalists, ferreting researchers and innovative home therapists!

My mantra: never assume, but read, read, read, and come to your own conclusions. Also, prepare and keep a file with all relevant reports from doctors, therapists, teachers and others. Keep a journal and record every little developmental milestone as well as food likes, dislikes or intolerances, and track triggers for behaviour, illnesses and wellbeing.

Charles Hart's book *A Parent's Guide to Autism*, starts with the following statement:

> To understand autism, or any other human condition, you must observe the individuals, not just the stereotypes. Our most talented teachers agree when they say: to reach a child with autism, you must first learn to see the world through the student's eyes.[12]

---

12   Hart, C. (1993) *A Parent's Guide to Autism*. New York, NY: Pocket Books, p.1

Charles Hart has a brother and a son with autism. As his brother was born around 1920, he did not have the intervention oppor-

tunities that are available now. Like Charles Hart, we are also glad that our son Michael was born in 1989 and not in 1920 or even in 1970. Each year seems to bring better services and better understanding of autism. But still – even today – the enigma remains.

When doing presentations, or talking about our life with autism, I like to use the analogy of travelling on a road. It can be a highway – often professionals appear to be travelling on a highway, like ruling lords, some haughty, others kind – or it can be a country road (where teachers and therapists are accompanying you along the way), or it can be a track, which we seem to be permanently travelling on, with potholes and other obstacles. All the roads are okay, and we can always turn off, or turn back, but we all have different roads that lead to different places, with major or minor roadworks along the way, all the way. We are influenced by the weather, the road conditions, other road users and obstacles we encounter en route. For example, we are influenced by professionals – and they are influenced by what and how they have learned – other parents, their experiences, teachers and their experiences and attitudes, society, accessibility to services and the family dynamics within our 'autism family'.

Michael was born in Harrismith in the Orange Free State in South Africa in March 1989. Everything seemed normal and we had a healthy baby. He was breastfed, but after two months he was started on solids as supplementary feed. Right from the start he seemed to lag behind in his development. From parents and friends we were getting the usual comments – he is just lazy, he is a boy, so-and-so only started this or that at whatever age. We had no experience with children and remained worried. Harrismith has no paediatrician, so on a home visit to Windhoek when Michael was 7 months old, I went to see one on the pretext that he was often constipated and that I'd like his milestones checked at the same time, as I had read in baby care books that such check-ups should be done regularly.

The doctor noticed some delays and suggested I see an occupational therapist. He also suspected a pulmonary stenosis, which was successfully treated at the University Hospital in Bloemfontein. With the help of a befriended occupational therapist with neuro-developmental therapy training, we searched for a diagnosis, while going ahead with general occupational therapy and physiotherapy. Michael did not like any weight on his arms – when we pulled him up by his fingers, he'd let go as soon as he felt some resistance, or had to work for himself. He also did not respond as expected to the frequency rattle, which is usually used during hearing assessments, but he would hear immediately if I stepped on the bottom step in our two-storey house, and he was extremely sensitive to the drawing of curtains or pulling of zips.

On our long and arduous journey in search of a diagnosis, we investigated and discarded many syndromes or illnesses, including autism, because Michael was an open and friendly baby, but through a friend we got back on the track of autism. Finally, we found our way to Unica School in Pretoria. Before we could have an assessment, a preliminary questionnaire consisting of 27 pages had to be filled in. There was an eight-month waiting list, as assessments with the whole team could only be carried out twice a month. After the assessment and the cautious diagnosis of mild autism, the Unica School team agreed to see us on an out-patient basis every two to three months, during which time we also received speech therapy ideas and psychological assistance.

The confirmation of the diagnosis of autism came as a shock but at least now we knew in which direction to head. All parents have dreams for their children, be it academic, musical, sporting or otherwise. It takes a while to get over the 'why me' question. Well, why someone else? Why at all? This is what this world is, and we cannot dwell on facts, we must look ahead and do something. Although professionals do not like to 'label' too early, at least one can start off in a direction. Thanks to understanding occupational therapists and physiotherapists, therapy was started early and included a lot of sensory integration exercises.

This went well until I came for assessment three weeks before the birth of our second child. I had not worked with Michael as much as I should have due to Round Table commitments and feeling big and heavy, and he had, between my last visit and then, not made much progress. We were informed that Michael would be put on the waiting list to be admitted to the kindergarten section of Unica School for 1993. Well, that came as a greater shock than the confirmation of the diagnosis of autism.

Put a three-year-old into boarding school? We found that an unacceptable idea, especially because Michael was such a lovable boy and not really a problem at home. What about the language? Our home language is German. Change it to English or Afrikaans? No – I found it too unnatural and it would make Michael feel even more of an outsider within the family and the home, which should be a secure and supportive unit. While we were living in Harrismith, he attended the regular English nursery school with Tryphina, his Sotho nanny. When we moved back to Namibia in 1994, I was lucky to find a young German lady who started off as an au pair but became my assistant and friend. She stayed for six years. Esther has been back to visit us a couple of times, and when she arrived, Michael would ignore her for a while as if punishing her for 'abandoning' him. After a day or three he would be fine, enjoying her company. After all these years, we are still in contact with Esther and Michael enjoys receiving photos from her via WhatsApp.

Over the years, we have had many volunteers, practitioners and assistants. They would go to school with Michael and work with him at home in the afternoon. They also helped with other children in the class after we found that he got lazy, for example expecting the volunteer to fetch his lunchbox at break time. The practitioners always worked in their field of study, so Michael received a cocktail of remedial teaching and special education, occupational therapy, physiotherapy, speech therapy and social skills training.

It is unfortunate that in Namibia, South Africa, as well as elsewhere in Africa, autism is still a fairly unknown entity among the population at large. We never hid Michael and always were prepared to discuss any questions people asked. We always informed people who were not so interested briefly, and had long conversations with interested parties. As active Round Tablers, we did a lot of travelling and Michael often came along, especially when he was younger. Often people probably thought I was a neurotic mother hen, but I did what I thought was right and I am glad about it. I bombarded my parents and parents-in-law with information to make them realise that Michael is who he is, and that the situation could get better through intervention but would never disappear. I maintain that the more we do now, the less we might have to do later. And if not, at least we will have tried to the best of our ability.

I do not know how I ended up receiving an invitation to go on an educational trip to Melbourne, Sydney and Auckland on the Citizen Ambassador Programme, where among others, I met Ruth Sullivan and Lois Blackwell and her daughter from the Judevine Centre. The trip was an eye-opener. Compared to Southern Africa, 'Down Under' appears to be a paradise with excellent programmes and opportunities. Travelling with and meeting so many professionals was an unforgettable experience.

I joined autism societies in South Africa, England, Germany, Belgium, America and Australia to see what the different approaches were. We adapted the information, therapy and methods to suit our needs. I read many accounts by autistic people or parents of autistic children. Through the internet, I now have contact with many parents and people with autism all over the world, gaining knowledge and thus being able to assist others whose journey has just started, or getting assistance from others who have been down the various paths already.

I enjoy attending conferences, as it is the only time when I am completely by myself and not responsible for anyone else, and not having to have two or more sets of ears and eyes. Whereas in the beginning I looked for intervention programmes and methods, nowadays I am interested in transition programmes, adult living options, and lifestyle planning.

I have collected so much material that we have a little library at Windhoek, headquarters of our organisation Autism Association of Namibia. Autism Association of Namibia is made up of parents, their children with ASD, adults with ASD, friends and professionals who are interested in promoting the wellbeing of persons with autism spectrum disorders within Namibia, and to provide a network between the various autism organisations world-wide. Our aim is to provide support and assistance as well as training in the field of autism to parents and professionals. In the current economic climate and with the diverse needs of various members of the community this is becoming increasingly difficult. We are busy categorising and listing and are embarking on an information network for Southern Africa and Africa in general, with abstracts of newsletters, books, medical material, and addresses of where to obtain things so that people can then order what they are interested in. What I am still looking for is a book of hints and tips for how others have coped or handled a specific situation. Of course, a lot of hints are found in books written by parents. For example, after reading Mary Callahan's book, *Fighting for Tony*,[13] I boiled Michael's milk for five minutes (I thought that boiling it for 20 would take any nutrients out of the milk) and thereafter he only woke up two or three times per night instead of eight times. After seeing Michael screaming every time he was given solids when he was 4 or 5 months old, a friend told me that her friend (who does not have an autistic child) fed all her babies while they were lying on their backs, and it worked with Michael as well. At about 8 months he was fed while leaning back in his pushchair and only when he was 9 or 10 months old could we feed him while sitting in a highchair.

With all the different programmes, therapies and medication available and each autistic individual being different, I believe that a tailor-made combination of therapies, vitamins, educational programmes, physical exercise and sensory integration will work the best in the long run. Force does not work. A person will only learn something when they are ready for it and not when *you* decide they are ready.

Different people have different interpretations of what a home

---

13   Callahan, M. (1987) *Fighting for Tony.* New York, NY: Fireside

programme is. To us it is a programme that is carried out mainly at home so that Michael can acquire the skills to function in society. This means that he should have some level of independence for toileting, dressing, eating, asking (or indicating) for help, road awareness, reading and writing, counting and leisure skills. Even if he does need to remain in supported living, there are some basic abilities that we'd like him to know and/or do. We have not restricted our aims and hopes to a certain level of functioning – learning is lifelong.

As it is so difficult to know what Michael's actual level of understanding is, we assume that he understands everything but we explain and show things over and over, until he masters them. What often amazes me is that he grasps some things much faster than others, especially if it is something that he fancies or that arouses his interest. On the one hand, it is good to have him at home and to be in charge of what he learns and how, but on the other hand, like any child, Michael does manipulate me and his other primary caregivers. At school with a teacher in a group situation, he might learn not to act in such a way. The other limitation was that with the home one-on-one training, by the age of 8 he had not learned to function in a group situation. He was also not interested in or able to imitate anything we did, either physically or vocally. Finally, after I imitated him for a very long time, often with us both facing a mirror, he realised that he could make me copy things that he did. By that time, he was about 9, and once he could imitate to a certain extent, life became far easier.

We are still implementing a home programme with Michael, but it changes. What is difficult to choose though, is whether to continue with self-help skills like dressing, when he is obviously so inept at fine motor skills. I have stopped forcing him to put on his own clothes, pack something away, help in the house and so on.

He is adept at many things that interest him, but when it comes to everyday functioning, he gets frustrated, which ends in stomping of feet and finger biting. When does one stop trying to teach and just let be, instead of having frustration every day?

When administering a home programme, it is vital that the child gets a professional assessment, which should be updated from time to time. It is important to make up your own file for the child and ask for and have copies of all correspondence in connection with assessments, programmes and medical histories. If a new professional has to work with the child, it is then easy to make copies of documents for that person. Once you have an assessment you will know at which level the child is functioning, in which area, and that forms the basis of the programme. You can determine what to concentrate on first but keep in mind the other areas of functioning so that the child does not fall behind in any of the others.

It is important to spend time with the siblings of an autistic child and to involve other family members in what you are trying to achieve. We have always been open about the diagnosis and many people do understand, while others don't. Often you will find that you have to cope with the non-acceptance of a diagnosis by close family members, for example a grandfather who cannot accept anything that is not perfect. You might have some members of family or friends who do not understand that a child's birthday party is no fun for your child. We will go, but I will ask beforehand that the host should excuse us if we need to leave early.

For shopping trips, it is difficult to take any child if you are a monthly shopper, so for these kinds of outings I have a very short list, like bread, bananas and milk, or just a newspaper or whatever. During the first years, we always had assistants and volunteers, so the children were used to different people.

At one stage, I could go out for an hour or so and leave the

TV on, or leave Michael in the garden, but these days he wants to be with us all the time, so outings to the pub mean that I have to teach him to drink his beer slowly, whereas when he was young, he had to empty his glass, so that it would not spill when falling over. He has to learn that two beers are enough and that he should drink water or a lemonade in between. He urgently needs a communication system, so that he can indicate when he needs to go to the bathroom; I can understand him – if he takes off his earphones while we are out it means he needs the bathroom – but his brother and father have had bad experiences with him as they did not 'read' him when he took off the earphones. It would be nice to find peers who will go with him, so that he is not constantly with older adults.

Through Unica School, we were introduced to the Start Programme, a wonderful and easy-to-use programme for children up to a developmental age of 3. It includes all the milestones in gross and fine motor, language and daily living skills. As Michael got older, the priorities changed and were adapted. Michael is now 27 but he functions at the level of a 2- to 7-year-old, so, in some ways, his development is at the tantrum age. Bad behaviour should not be seen as bad behaviour, as usually it is due to a lack in communication skills. It is understandable that he might become rebellious and we have had to work around that, as we would with any 2-year-old. However, we do not treat Michael like a baby. We have always used normal speech with him. In time, we began to be able to see if something was way beyond his level and we would start again or explain something in easier language. I have also tried to teach both our children sharing and acceptance of one another. Michael often started crying at the kindergarten when he saw me. It took quite a while before I realised that he cried because I was wearing sunglasses when I arrived. Or he would sit down and scream his head off. I was more tuned in to him and realised that he was jealous if his brother greeted me first. He was used to greeting me first. So, I have explained to him that I have two children and that each of them has the same right. He still gets very upset if I come to school to pick him up early and go and see the headmaster, so I am not at the car when he comes and that makes him cross. We realised that he was able to understand most of what we said, if we used short sentences and plain language.

It is important to *listen* to your child. At all times, I try to be aware of what is going on around me, so that I can reply to Michael if he 'says' something. While driving, I am always commenting on this, that or the other. Suddenly he might say, 'yoiyoi'. Looking in the rear-view mirror I see a truck has passed and I reply, 'Yes, Michael, that was a red truck with bricks, or tipper truck or big yellow truck with cattle.' Or he gets very excited. I realise that there are lots of treetops or telephone cables around and I say, 'Yes, Michael, there are many telephone/electricity cables/pylons.' And I also *listen* to his distress signals, when he suddenly gets upset and closes his ears. Is there a siren, does the open car window bother him, or his screaming brother, or a whiny escalator, or a vibrating fridge, or the air-conditioning, or a plane that has flown overhead? At home, I get down on the floor with him and look at and comment on his ants or insects and do the same as he does. He appreciates me playing 'his' games. If he does not want to do something, I do not just pull him along, but explain to him why he has to do this or that. I talk and explain at all times, even if he does not seem to hear me.

One big advantage that we have now is that Michael understands the concept of 'first this, then that' – first we have to work and then you can play with your string, or twirl the rings on the floor, or whatever stimming action he prefers. If I promise something, I keep to my promise, so that Michael gets used to the fact that my if/then condition is true. And I also try to remember to praise him, even for the effort of just trying something. Praise should be over-emphasised and happen often, although we might have to fade over-praising later, as in real life it is not the norm to be praised after every little effort.

We have come to the realisation that augmentative and alternative communication should have been used consistently a long time ago and right from the beginning. It is never too late, and we are currently implementing a system.

We have been doing a disservice to Michael in not meeting his overall communication needs. Being able to communicate with the primary caregiver only is not enough. There are excellent sites, information, programmes and apps on communication and literacy.

I cannot say that we have gone for one particular programme. At the beginning, it was occupational therapy and physiotherapy and the Start Programme. I read as much as I can, and I subscribe to many autism magazines and newsletters. I find accounts of people with autism of particular interest, as this gives me an indication of how their minds work. As I read more, I include parts of other programmes/therapies which I think might work. One should not chop and change continuously, as often it takes a bit longer before you can see the benefit of a therapy. As those with autism mostly do not like change, even if they are not ritualistic, it might take a while before they get used to and accept a programme. Michael often does not like to try something because he does not understand what is expected of him or what the game/programme entails, but after we have followed something through consistently, he will be happier to go along with us.

Right from the start we have used sensory integration therapy, including things like stroking the dog's or cat's fur, explaining sensations such as rough, soft, smooth, cold, warm and bristly. Michael is still mouthing a lot and chewing his T-shirts with his tongue or sticking his fingers in his mouth and biting his fingers.

To me, this seems to mean that he needs even more stimulation around the mouth and mouth exercises, and also finger pressure and massage and fine motor activities. Today, sensory integration is still necessary. Massage is good and exercises to improve body awareness are still very important.

Work on fine motor skills is very necessary, and being outdoors and riding therapy are still great fun.

I have never forced my children to eat something they did not like, but I don't agree with children saying they don't like something before trying it, or because father, mother or whoever does not like it. So, we accepted if Michael refused something, but always tried again. We didn't try extremes like very hot or very sour, because I felt that he might lose confidence in us. During the last three months, Michael has been far more adventurous with food, which we think has a lot to do with the sensory integration programme. He has learned to eat lettuce, cucumber, carrots and more; sometimes he actually requests (points) to something like salad, but still without dressing, and still no sour items. He is becoming more adventurous with condiments. When introducing 'new' food, I still make him try at least one bite or spoonful, accepting his decision on eating more or declining.

Until he was about 12, we implemented the following programme: at the beginning Michael had to work for five minutes and play for ten minutes. The aim was to lengthen the working time and lessen the playing time as his concentration ability improved. We also varied the programme, so that he did not get bored. The activities also varied according to his health and mood. Some days we could do more, other days it was less.

Whatever programme you develop, it should balance physical with intellectual exercises, and integrated in the whole set-up are dressing, toileting, washing, eating, and other socially interactive activities. The workplace should be a room or part of the room where the child knows that work is expected of him, although I have used any place, including the kitchen floor or toilet, for incidental teaching. We store our *National Geographic* magazines in the bathroom and these are a great source for teaching about ordinary things like mountains, water, animals, fire, plants and people. It is important to remember that learning is lifelong. Michael has his own way of completing a puzzle. He has outgrown the 12–20-piece puzzles, slowly working his way up to 150 pieces. He enjoys looking at picture books, increasing his receptive vocabulary, and we learn 'his' pronunciation of words. He is now showing an interest in letters, so maybe he is ready to learn to read.

Ideally, two people should be able to do these programmes (teaching him to return a ball, or bat a ball), but this is not always possible. Over the last few years we have had many assistants and helpers. It takes a lot of time to train them and then they go, or they don't really have the interest. It can be disruptive to continually have strangers in your house. We are lucky that we could afford to have an assistant for Michael who goes to kindergarten with him and is also available to help out at weekends. One thing to look out for is a person who is not afraid to crawl around the floor with your child, or babble in his language, someone who really is interested in him and interacts with him.

Even as an adult, Michael is not interested in working independently. Working without assistants at this stage is not possible, so we always need someone, even if it is for certain hours of the day only. He does want to learn, and it is good to see him happy to work after a weekend or holidays, when the staff come back. So far, our programme and our curriculum have been working quite well, and at present there are still no autism-specific services in Namibia.

Now, at the age of 27, Michael's needs are changing and as an adult the emphasis is more on daily life skills rather than academic skills. Shortly, we aim to start an adult activity centre, maybe once a week to start off with, building up to more days. Fundraising must be done to employ a full-time occupational therapist to manage the programme. As we have no government support whatsoever, any service that is set up or offered by the private sector is relatively expensive.

At all times, our minds must remain open for new avenues of thinking and we must re-programme our aims and expectations, always reminding ourselves of how our child will cope once we are no longer there to help and assist him. Any typical child will leave home after school to study, to marry, to leave the nest, so we should aim for our children to be able to live their own lives after they are 18 or 25, be it in a fairly normal environment or a sheltered home or whatever.

Of course, we also wonder what will happen to Michael or what his prospects are, but, in the meantime, we look ahead, work with what we've got and try and help him to understand this world. We cannot change the past and therefore we must try and make the best of the future.

What I would have done differently? I did the best I could with what I had at the time. The only thing I would do differently is start with augmentative and alternative communication right from the start – to give a voice to those who don't have a voice. Communication does not have to be speech as we know it.

And I would have taught some things to Michael as I would to an adult. For example, it might be okay for the child to relieve himself in the garden because it takes to long to get to the toilet when the child is 2 or even 4, but it is embarrassing when the 'child' is 14 or 24. Whatever you teach your child, if it is okay in the baby/toddler phase but not later, you will have to spend unnecessary time retraining them later.

At the Autism Association of Namibia, we are using the

approaches we have used with Michael to educate and inform children with autism spectrum disorders, as well as their parents, carers, teachers, and professionals in our sparsely populated country with a multitude of cultures and traditions. As we grow, we learn, and we will adapt our programme and share with the others the updated information.

All children and people learn, some faster, some slower. Learning is lifelong. Never chastise yourself or your family for not having done this, that or the other. Don't attempt to overcome all with expensive therapies. Work out a home programme with your occupational therapist and your speech therapist and teachers. Do an individualised education plan for the various stages of the child's life and update it every now and then. Let the child do the 'leading' in terms of when they are ready for the next item to learn. Gently nudge, build confidence and try out new things. Forcing something will only result in a regression because of fear or lack of readiness.

Take time out to recharge your batteries. Loving and laughing with autism will show you little stories to let you know that you are not alone. It isn't a train smash when things don't work out as you planned.

Refrigerator mothers? Sometimes, because you need to retreat into this cocoon of ice to cool off when yet another person does not want to understand *how* to teach your child, *how* to speak to your child, or when a family member once again thinks the child just needs a good spanking (even in these days when spanking is definitely out). We need to refrigerate and ice up to be able to cope and reach out and manage the next day.

In the same way, autistic people aren't in a bubble on their own. Recent research has proven that they have empathy and feelings and emotions but experience or show them in different ways. We knew that, didn't we? Go with your gut feeling! Empirical evidence proves this, that or the other depending on which variables you take into consideration, but life as we live it is the true experience and the true marker for our road.

Therefore, in between being an investigative forensic journalist, a ferreting researcher and an innovative home therapist, do not forget to enjoy life and your family!

Chapter 12

SAMIRA AND FATIMA

(KUWAIT)

When a woman has her third child, she thinks she's the expert mum in raising children! But, this was not my feeling when I had Fatima. How did I miss that she communicated differently from my other older kids? How did I not notice that she cried more than they did? Every time I found an excuse for the situation or the different behaviour, until she was obviously not talking or communicating to us as she did to her dolls when she was 3 years old. This  is when we started our journey to the doctors! Some said she was deaf, others said she was mentally retarded or jealous of her sister.

When she reached 5 years old, we heard the word 'autism' for the first time. But we thought that maybe the doctors were mistaken in their diagnosis, so we travelled and took her to another hospital in the USA, but the word 'autism' came up again and we were pushed into a new world.

We went back to Kuwait with 20 books about autism to try to understand more, as we were told that there was no miracle medicine for autism.

In our attempts to find a suitable school, I let her join a special classroom with four other different handicapped children, but she didn't learn much. Her tantrums were increasing, because we couldn't understand what she wanted. She isolated herself with her toys and books.

After a difficult year when I had my fourth child as well as having a serious operation that forced me to stay in bed for long months, we decided to give Fatima three to four years of our lives by moving to the USA and leaving my older son and daughter with my mother in Kuwait.

We stayed in Boulder for a year and then we moved to Boston as we heard that schools for autism were much more developed there. During our 'mission', we were ready to sacrifice anything to provide Fatima with the necessary education and to go back home with some experience to help her.

We found that we were not alone as we received more and more calls from people in Kuwait who we didn't even know, enquiring about autism, what Fatima learned at school in the USA and whether we would recommend it for their son or daughter. Even our late President, Sheikh Jaber Al-Sabah, when my husband went to him to ask permission to leave his job as Undersecretary for three to four years, said, 'Then that is your mission with your wife, to learn and come back to Kuwait to help others like your daughter.' At that time, we didn't know that this might happen, but it did!

As I attended lectures or conferences for autism, my husband encouraged me to continue with my Master's in Special Education and join the programmes for autism at Boston College and Lesley College, where, ultimately, I learned a lot, especially during the practical sessions. I benefited mainly from the comparison between the one-to-one American way in the most famous schools in Boston and the Japanese Higashi School system, where there were several children in the class.

I was the first teacher to be trained in the school and I learned a lot from Dr Kiyo Kitahara's 'daily life therapy' programme, with hands-on management. What I found was that many programmes have similar basic ideas but with different names! The most successful ingredients for a programme are dedicated, loving and caring teachers to translate the theory into practice and promote progress for the children.

Fatima started writing and counting and became more independent, as well as learning to play the harmonica! What a big achievement! When she started, she wouldn't sit on a chair for more than a few seconds but as time went by, she stayed fully focused until 3.20pm – the whole school day.

We were happy, but we knew we needed to plan for the future. Should we live in the USA as our daughter was progressing so well, or should we go back to Kuwait to develop something for her there? After much communication with my mother and family, we decided to go back to Kuwait, hoping for the best for our daughter.

When we returned to Kuwait in 1988, I started a small classroom for her at home with two other children with autism and they did very well. During this time, my husband had to go to Saudi Arabia as he was appointed to a government job for four years. After a month, we decided to visit him as it was the summer vacation. When we had been there three days, Iraq invaded Kuwait and we couldn't go back to our country!

A lot of our family and friends who escaped from the occupation visited us in Saudi Arabia, so our home was always full of people during that period; it was noisy and there was not much quiet time for Fatima. After the Liberation of Kuwait in 1991, we decided to stay with my husband in Saudi Arabia for another three years. I opened a classroom for Fatima and three others with autism at my other home in Saudi Arabia, and in 1992 I published my first book about autism, which was the first book on this subject in an Arabic language. From the feedback I received by mail and from visitors, I learned that autism was affecting the lives of many more children than I had realised. A year later, I was contacted by the Women's Society in Jeddah, Saudi Arabia, and asked to open a school for autism, which we successfully did in 1993. I chose the name Friends' School, as people with autism lack the ability to communicate and they need friends, but later the name was changed to the Jeddah Centre for Autism. Since then it has become well known in Saudi Arabia.

At the same time, I tried to establish the same programme in Kuwait and my husband used his influence to convince responsible officers in the government. In 1993, the project was accepted by the Awqaf Public Foundation to provide us with the legal structure to raise funds, as from the beginning I didn't want it to be just a private school. My dream was to have a non-profit organisation, having a bigger mission than just a school. In 1994, the programme started in Kuwait in a leased building not originally intended for a school.

I began the first four months with training and giving all theoretical information needed for the teachers. Then we enrolled five students. The second year, people knew about the centre and started applying to send their children. At first, we couldn't accept all the children, as every teacher works with two or three students only, but from six students in the first year, we have now reached 130 students with 75 teachers, occupational therapists and speech therapists!

Any extra budget I got, I used to invite professionals whom I met all over the world at conferences or during my studies, to give parents, teachers and doctors in Kuwait the chance to listen to them. Some were the authors of famous theories such as Eric Schopler and Gary Mesibov (*Structured Teaching – The TEACCH method*), Tony Attwood (*The Complete Guide to Asperger's Syndrome*), Margaret Walker (*MAKATON Symbols*), Theo Peeters (*Autism: Medical and Educational Aspects*), Booney Vance (*Psychological Assessment of Children*) and many others.

My Fatima grew up with the development of the centre. I tried to see what she needed as an example of our needs in the programme. To be sure of the effectiveness of the programme, I sought accreditation and ISO (International Organisation for Standardisation) certification, which we received. Furthermore, the most important task was to record the whole system of the Centre (administration and students' curriculum) to ensure the transfer of knowledge so that anyone could access it and continue our work.

Sixteen years ago, we started a model for students over the age of 21 and I called it Youth House. Young adults with autism come at 11am and leave at 6pm. They spend their day engaging in job training, visits within the community, leisure activities, buying groceries and cooking their lunch. Then at 6pm they go back to their parents as I don't believe in residential programmes except for urgent cases. I believe these young people should live with their families, even for a short time, so at the end of the day their mothers can tuck them into bed. As we get the land for our Youth Project and attract sponsors, we will be able to build and so our dream to be able to cater for young people with autism over the age of 18 years will come true.

The mission of love, care and learning about autism will never end, but we live it day by day and thank God for all he has given us.

Chapter 13

SHUBHANGI AND VISHU

(INDIA)

Writing about my son, Vishu, and my journey with him opens up the floodgates of memory; after all, hasn't he dominated my every waking moment for the past several years? Haven't all my plans, projects and decisions centred around his life and needs? Hasn't my identity as an 'autism mother' become a defining one in my life? As he celebrates his 20th birthday, and I my 51st, it is time for me to take a step back and look at the unique individual he has become, rather than a part of the mother–child dyad that people with disabilities are frequently locked into.

Autism mothers have played a major role in shaping discourses around the condition, challenging the archaic and sexist narrative of the 'refrigerator mother', becoming activists and advocates for their children, and making significant academic and research contributions to advancing our knowledge about autism. In India, as in the rest of the world, mothers have been on the frontlines; if not refrigerator mums, they have nevertheless been cast as incompetent ones, incapable of raising a 'normal' child, blamed and ridiculed by family and community alike. Mothers in India have also challenged these stereotypes by becoming agents of social change, creating awareness and services, mobilising the community and literally giving birth to autism activism. As an autism mum, I too have been a part of this movement; as a researcher in sociology I have attempted to make visible the issues and challenges confronting families like mine within academic discourses around disability in India.

Attempting to be the 'voices' that represent our children, we also run the risk of appropriating them, viewing them as extensions of ourselves, rather than as individuals with their own stories. Autistic children grow up into autistic adults. While we know that this statement is true, we still find it easier to think of the autistic person as a permanent child whose decisions and choices are ours to make. This is particularly the case in family-centric cultures like mine, where even neurotypical adults defer to the wishes and decisions of parents and other family members in matters ranging from career choice to marriage partners. Writing about my young adult with autism and representing him as the young man he has become rather than the child I have raised, promises to be both challenging and liberating.

Vishu came into my life on a spring day in 1997, two years and two months after the birth of his older brother. His father and I joked about how we would manage the stress of the 'Board Exams', as our little boys would be in Grades 10 and 12 in the same year! (The 'Board Exams' are a rite of passage for school kids in India, determining their prospects in higher education, and a source of immense tension for the exam-taker and family alike.) Of course, we had no way of knowing the different trajectories their lives would take; our older boy went through the much-valued urban middle-class Indian route of public school and university, while Vishu attended a centre for children with autism and never went to a 'mainstream' school.

Being second-time parents, we were quick to pick up the differences in his developmental path. We realised that our active, inquisitive little boy was far more interested in objects than people (except for Mommy); he had strange, inexplicable fears and fascinations; he developed  speech late and his first words were extremely unusual; he was unresponsive to his name, did not point or make gestures, and had occasional fearsome tantrums that left us all exhausted and utterly bewildered. The autism diagnosis was devastating, of course, but paradoxically a relief as well, because we realised that there were other people like him, and families like ours; that early intervention and teaching methods geared towards helping him cope with his difficulties would certainly yield results. We were extremely lucky to get an early diagnosis and find suitable services. A decade and a half ago, autism spectrum disorder was still a marginal and relatively unknown condition in India; the absence of specialist services and the reluctance of mainstream schools to admit kids who were 'different' often resulted in them being closeted at home or having a difficult time in settings where their unique needs and subjectivities were neither acknowledged nor understood.

Further upheavals were to visit our family. My husband passed away suddenly and tragically, when the boys were still very small, forcing us to regroup and pick up the shattered pieces of our lives. Life as a single mother with two young kids was never going to be easy, especially when one of the kids had a diagnosis of autism. However, my child found a place in Open Door School, a model school for children with autism in Delhi. Run by the parent-driven non-profit organisation Action for Autism, which pioneered the nascent autism movement in India, Open Door truly opened up a new world of possibilities for my son and, indeed, our family. It was here that the volatile, hyperactive child with a well-earned reputation as a habitual 'runner' settled down over the years to become an eager and enthusiastic learner, a talented painter and a versatile performer in the annual school plays. I benefited greatly from the workshops and parent trainings regularly conducted there and had the opportunity to attend lectures and workshops by autism experts from across the world. I also networked with other families like mine, becoming part of a larger community cutting across geographical borders, bound by a common circumstance and facing similar challenges.

Surrounded by people who love and accept him unconditionally for the person that he is, Vishu has grown into a confident young adult with a strong sense of self, an interest in meeting people and visiting new places, a great sense of fun and enjoyment, and a love of good food, music and stylish clothing. He is a wonderful chap to hang out with. Unfussy, and quite happy to rough it (provided there is good food at the end of the road), he is a good travel companion. One year, the two of us embarked on a week-long exploration of the historical delights of our city, Delhi. Rediscovering the familiar is as fascinating as exploring the unknown, and Delhi in winter has a special kind of magic. We walked through the congested streets of Old Delhi, sampling its culinary delights, marvelled at the architectural splendours of the massive Red Fort, Qutub Minar, and the tombs of Safdar Jung and Emperor Humayun, soaked in the serene majesty of the magnificent Jama Masjid and stumbled on lesser known but equally marvellous structures from different periods in Delhi's layered past. We visited the Nehru Memorial Museum and pored over the black and white photographs that marked our great freedom struggle, then later ate out at the international food chains that mark a new sort of colonial takeover!

Exploring our great city, we rediscovered each other too. I noted that the impulsive little boy who ran like the wind and could not be left unattended for a second would look out for me and ensure that I did not get lost in the teeming city and chaotic traffic. It was he who would envelop my small hand in his massive, manly one and marshal me through crowded streets. Big, burly and imposing in appearance, he made me feel safe and secure. While he continued to be fascinated by the wheels of cars and buses, he was considerably more circumspect about diving beneath vehicles to explore their workings!

We walked for miles in the winter sun, hopped in and out of Metro trains and buses and behaved like tourists in a new city. Vishu took many photographs on his mobile phone, not just of the iconic monuments, but also of the shops in the heart of Delhi trading in iron tools and chainsaws, the electric transmission towers, floodlights and street lights whose symmetrical lines, I must concede, embodied a certain beauty that seemed to resonate with him. Indeed, no object was too trivial or mundane; his undisguised delight and appreciation of the things that caught his fancy did lead to a few curious stares and raised eyebrows by passers-by, but more often than not these changed to hesitant smiles and friendly nods. We also spent a couple of magical evenings attending the Indian classical music concerts that are a regular feature of the city's cultural scene, in massive public auditoriums packed to the rafters with music lovers young and old. Vishu listened, entranced, to elaborate 'ragas' (compositions) both vocal and instrumental with eyes tightly shut and a huge smile on his face; if there had been space, I knew he would have loved to whirl round and round, feeling the rhythm and melody become part of his body.

Our 'Discover Delhi' adventures made me deeply aware of how far he has come in his own journey, how much more connected and comfortable he is with the world around him, and how happy he is being the person he is. While still more dependent on me than other young men of his age, he nevertheless comes across as being a smart and confident young person. He negotiates public spaces swiftly and surely, asks for help when he needs it and is not afraid of anybody. Like a true blue 'Dilli da Munda' (Delhi lad), he thrusts his way through crowds, has a ready temper, and an equally hearty laugh. The Delhi Metro railway network fascinates him, and he loves examining the route map. He negotiates airports, malls and any system with clear signage with ease. He takes to technology like a duck to water and loves to keep pace with it. He is adept at operating all the gizmos without which life as we know it cannot go on, and is my go-to guy when the computer acts funny or the smartphone leaves me feeling very stupid! He is, truly, a citizen of a new world, a new century. In that sense, he is far more at home in it than his technologically challenged mother who grew up in simpler times.

The challenges that his condition poses, of course, cannot be denied, and like every autism parent in the world I worry about his future when I am gone. In countries like India, the traditional support networks for the elderly, the disabled and other vulnerable populations are rapidly eroding due to the sweep of industrialisation, urbanisation and migration. However, social security services, residential care and other systems common in the Global North have yet to emerge here. But thanks to the activism of families and other stakeholders, new avenues and opportunities are emerging. My dream for Vishu and other people like him is that they will be able to live productively in communities where they receive the support and scaffolding that they need, while contributing to their maximum potential. Communities based on mutual cooperation and interdependence, not charity and doles, premised on the dignity of every human being, irrespective of (dis)ability.

When Vishu was very little I asked his teacher in anguish, 'Will he ever get married? Will he ever have friends?' She gently replied that he might, or he might not, and that the things that mattered so much to me, may not matter in the same way to him, because he would be a person in his own right. At 20, Vishu has many friends. Some are the buddies he has grown up with; some are adults much older than him with whom he has struck up a great rapport and understanding; one of his most loyal friends is his 'Aunty', a caregiver who looked after the children when they were little but refuses to 'leave' the job because she is so attached to Vishu. Together they watch TV, chat, have tea and enjoy each other's company. He wants to get married someday. He knows that to do so, he will need to earn his living and find a partner who will also want to share life with him. So yes, he does have friends and he may even marry. But that is because of his will and desire and not my dreams and wishes.

A few years ago, we had a bit of a mix-up on the Metro line that Vishu loves to travel on. He stepped into the train without me, and to my horror, the train left the station. With a pounding heart, I boarded the next train. Our destination was a few stops away, and the ten-minute journey seemed like an eternity. As the train pulled into the station, I noticed a solitary figure in jeans and a green sweater anxiously waiting on the platform. When I disembarked, he ran towards me, and hugged me. 'Mom! I thought you were lost!' he cried out. My little boy has now grown up; we have in fact found each other.

Chapter 14

STEPHANIE AND FRANK

(ENGLAND)

I feel an overwhelming sadness as I start to write this. A lump in my throat and misty eyes, I'm gazing at the screen and in my head trying to find the positives that I want to tell you about, but I guess like many parents there are more flashes of the situations that went wrong than the joys and fun, and somehow the anger and frustration that I thought had long gone tightens my chest.

I have drafted some notes and I am trying to make this interesting – a reflection of the ups and downs – but what appears on paper is the lifelong commitment, and constant worry that a parent with a child with autism will make.

I'm not a birth mum, I'm a foster mum. Frank, now aged 41, was fostered by us when he was just 5 years old. Frank is here on his regular weekend visits, that have happened since my husband died nearly six years ago. We've just been sitting at the kitchen table; I've asked Frank's permission to write something and he says fine, although I'm not sure he understands that other people will be reading this. I tried to trawl through his memories and I am reminded how tough life is for him – still.

Does he have friends? 'No.'

How does he think he is coping? 'Okay. I'm not scared any more, but my heart still thumps.'

Does the medication (Clozapine) help? 'No, not really. I just feel sick and it's hard to think. I just go blank.'

What about the future, what would he like to try? 'I can't see a future.'

What does he remember from the past? 'Not much.'

Does a diagnosis help? 'Yes, saying I'm schizophrenic means I'm mad, but saying I have autism spectrum disorder means I like things done in a certain way and I'm best left alone.'

We talk for a while, then Frank usually sits for hours over endless cups of tea, from about 9am to 11am, until I shout for him to do something. Occasionally I'll leave him sleeping rather than deal with his docile non-communicative behaviour. On good days, I'm sympathetic and understand his difficulty in starting any tasks. On other days, I get irritated. He has a fixation about the curved drive and disappears into the spare bedroom to look out of the venetian blinds at the shape of the road. He has a phobia about the police (from when he was sectioned) and when we are sweeping in the garden, he frequently goes into the front garden to check that there is no police car in the road. He likes to feel enclosed – 'in my own space and time' – and chooses to sleep in the gym shed at the bottom of the garden. It's freezing, but he feels safe there. Being cold is preferable to being hot.

Now at 41, his social anxiety is fuelled by anticipatory thoughts. He knows these thoughts are called 'catastrophic thinking', as this is from the last training at the job centre, which should have helped him get into the world of work. At the end of the course, one telephone interview with a theme park didn't result in a job offer. Then a friend suggested an evening cleaning job from 7pm to 9pm.

Perfect, no one is around, he can daydream while he cleans, and he hasn't missed a day in 16 months of work. This seems a waste of skills, as I can see him working at a call centre because he has a very good phone manner. Friends comment that they have spoken to Frank when I'm out and had a chat.

I still struggle to say that all of this is okay. I try to see the positives: that he has a job, that he can help me in the house and garden, and he is a kind, softly spoken, caring person. But like lots of real mums, I wish that some things were different and he was happier. I worry about how he will cope when I die. I guess like lots of mums, the experience of living and knowing an adult with autism is best described as a picture of heightened anxiety for both of us. As well as his mental distress seen in periods of depression, anxiety impacts on his physical body causing bowel problems, fatigue and insomnia. The blond-haired boy with blue eyes is now a middle-aged man with high blood pressure, back pain and stomach disorders.

Even as a foster parent, I feel a sense of failure that my husband and I were unable to make it right for him, that in some way our care didn't help. This I know is nonsense, but because Frank didn't receive a diagnosis of autism spectrum disorder until he was 14 years old, we responded to the many suggestions that were put forward to us by well-meaning social workers and professionals, and there was always a feeling that we might be the cause of his behaviour rather than there being an attempt made between us to make sense of his behaviour.

Initially we agreed with his social worker in making a story of loss. Frank had addictive parents, was identified as a baby that 'failed to thrive', and sadly was abused by a babysitter. Because these terrible experiences were seen as the cause of his behaviour, the lack of imaginative play, poor communication and social anxiety were regarded as being caused by other factors. At the time, I thought he was too bright to be autistic. Now that I understand autism as a spectrum disorder, I realise that this might have helped us in being able to describe his level of distress. As a young child, Frank missed out on some of the excellent strategies, now used in schools, that might have helped.

When Frank stays with me, we write lists of jobs to do, and give each other a bit of praise for jobs well done. We agree on the time for supper and what to watch on TV. I put sticky notes on the radio – 'Turn it off' – and in the bathroom – 'Do not stay in the shower for more than five minutes.' A trip to the cinema to see a favourite actor is prepared in advance. He keeps his hood up and carries the car keys in case he needs to exit for some reason.

Why do I do this? It's simple, I like to see him looking more relaxed and less anxious. When I'm tired and irritable, or forget his struggles, I can see an increase in his phobias, hand washing and showering. He believes he gives off an odour and people can smell him, so he constantly sprays his body with cheap deodorant. This is true, because when he's stressed he sweats, his hands are sticky and his breath pungent, like old iron.

Frank had been due to come for two weeks over the Christmas period in 1981, to give his mum a break. We visited his home and when his mum's boyfriend asked him to light a cigarette and then hauled him up and hung him from a hook behind the kitchen door for fun, we knew that this was going to be a damaged little boy. My husband said no, but my heart melted, and I thought we could offer something for the two-week holiday period.

Frank arrived on a Saturday, two days before Christmas, with the on-duty social worker. He was wearing plimsoles, but had no coat, and she carried two plastic bags that contained unwashed clothes that were too small. We panicked and took this frightened little boy shopping. He ran around the shop, screamed when we tried to fit sturdier shoes and couldn't be placated. He cringed when we tried to hold his hand and he shouted and swore. We quickly abandoned trying to explain the shopping trip and gathered up some new clothing from Woolworths and headed home. We had no words to explain except to say, 'It's a holiday.' After tea and a bath, Frank sat on the stairs saying, 'stupid holiday, stupid holiday'. He used the 'f' word a lot. I can remember once being asked by a headteacher if my husband swore at home as this might account for his bad language.

We made sense of Frank's behaviour in the context of a distressed child separated from his mum. We changed the plans for walking and playing to quietly sitting. Frank ran from room to room, charged around the garden, screamed, fell to the floor. We wanted to hold him and stop him but made sense of this behaviour by agreeing that we were looking after a distressed, abandoned child.

The two weeks came and went, and a newly allocated social worker asked if we could look after Frank for a longer period, perhaps a few months. We received a phone call from the headteacher of his primary school. She had recommended that Frank continued to be fostered and filled in the background of a boy who had 'failed to thrive' and had been hospitalised for 'not eating' and who displayed 'extreme distress'. He had spent two years in an opportunity class nursery (nurture group) but they hadn't seen very much progress. She thought he had ADHD.

We were teachers, so this made sense – attention deficit hyper-activity disorder. No wonder he ran around, couldn't concentrate and fiddled a lot. We felt we could work with him and had lots of ideas. We loved walking, swimming and cycling, and could offer both physical and learning activities. Football became his game of choice and he played with my husband for hours, kicking the ball up and down, but never improving or displaying much skill.

We noticed that his ears were discharging and that his breath was always stale. He burped a lot, and we thought he might have been copying his mum's boyfriend, but now later realised that he probably had gastric reflux. He now takes indigestion tablets every day.

We tackled some of the health problems. A hearing loss which was confirmed by our GP, who organised for grommets to be fitted. We were told that his ears were very sore and several back teeth were rotten. Why hadn't Frank told us? How did he manage with the pain? Research tells us that unrecognised pain can be a cause of challenging behaviours.[14]

At no point did we think 'autism', as Frank was too bright. His language was improving, his could write his name, he liked sums. But managing his behaviour was tough. We were seen in the local swimming pool by another social worker who reported us for roughly handling Frank. My husband was pulling him out of the water for trying to strangle a little girl while I tried to explain to an irate mother that he found it hard to cope. We had been

---

14 Knoll, A.K.I., McMurtry, C.M. and Chambers, C.T. (2013) 'Pain in children with Autism Spectrum Disorder: Experience, expression and assessment.' Paediatric Pain Letter: August 2013 Vol 15 No 2, 23–28; Bandstra, N.F. *et al.* (2012) 'Self-reported and parent-reported pain for common painful events in high functioning children and adolescents with autism.' *Clinical Journal of Pain 2012, 28, 715–721*

observed to be strict foster parents at the regular social play events. We dreaded these as Frank ran out of control, knocking into other children and becoming overwhelmed. Our attempts to call him to us failed, and to get him to stop we would have to grab him.

Margaret Golding wrote on our behalf to the head of social services and a case conference started the ball rolling in getting more help. An educational psychologist confirmed ADHD and maladjusted behaviour and Frank was referred to a local special school that had a unit for children with emotional and behavioural difficulties (EBD). This was a great setting, with just six children in the class and a sympathetic teacher who showed a genuine interest in his obsessions. Margaret had also suggested that psychotherapy or play therapy might help Frank deal with his disturbed and chaotic background, and this was agreed by social services.

We went as a family to the first sessions, but as Frank started to play with the toys, all hell broke loose and everything went up in the air. We watched and cried, but the psychotherapist was reassuring. After three weeks, we waited while Frank went in for his session. Eventually she said that she felt Frank needed a long-term intervention and at least two years of therapy. The results of this therapy are evident in his conversation and he can now explain the reasons why he was fostered while other children stayed at home.

Unexpectedly, this little boy became central to our lives and we felt we needed to commit ourselves to him. The fostering plan changed and we became his long-term foster parents, with his mother having weekly visits.

Life started to settle when my husband agreed to delay starting a new job to be at home with Frank for three months. The morning routine was calmer. Without realising, we were starting to put a TEACCH (Treatment and Education of Autistic and related Communication handicapped Children)-type programme in place. Up at the same time, wash, clean teeth – paste put on the brush beforehand – dress from a basket, then floor play with a ten-minute timer. Breakfast and then in the taxi to school. A wonderful driver took Frank to school every day for five years and added to the security and continuity that he needed. Somehow the driver knew to use sensible phrases like, 'I'm not listening to shouting or swearing' and 'Tell me when you're ready to talk.'

When my husband returned to work, we employed a new cleaner-cum-childminder. This brilliant lady introduced a restricted language code that worked – 'stop, no, do it now', and it did the trick. As new strategies came into my teaching job, I learned about 'now/then/finish', but at the time these simple commands that she used worked and stopped us getting into long and pointless discussions or arguments.

The first psychotherapy report identified Frank as a little boy with psychotic behaviour and his condition was described as 'childhood schizophrenia'. It was many years later when I met Dr O'Gorman that I remembered this was the original term used for autism. Still we didn't make sense of what we were being told. Another case conference suggested that he should go to a residential boarding school, but we wanted him to be with us.

As time went on, we were becoming more 'autistic-like' in our own behaviour. Visits to foster grandparents, who found Frank difficult to manage, were reduced. Holidays were always the same – a visit to a cottage in the Pennines, in the middle of nowhere. There were no big presents, only small items, wrapped in lots of paper that could be torn off. We had a routine of walking until we were exhausted and then snoozing in front of the fire, followed by table football and, when he was older, table tennis. His favourite foods were fish fingers, but no fruit or anything that was hard to bite. All labels were cut out of clothing. Even now Frank wears his T-shirts inside out and when I remind him he makes some excuse for not realising he's put it on the wrong way. I thought occupational therapists dealt with the elderly, and it never occurred to me that they would help with some of the sensory processing that was problematic. Friends slowly disappeared, and we didn't get invited to dinner parties.

From the age of 7, Frank was never invited to tea or to play. Thankfully we had an incredible cat who didn't mind being picked up and put into a pram and wheeled around the field at the back of the garden, and this brought little girls to the door who also mothered Frank. A springer spaniel, Bronte, who would play ball for hours enticed some boys to our door, and Frank could be part of this gang.

A lovely American woman phoned me to say she had a son with some special needs, who was also withdrawn; she had noticed Frank and wondered if they could be play-buddies. They had a computer, and Frank and Paul would sit at it for hours playing Pokémon. They developed a sympathetic friendship and enjoyed each other's company. Sadly, they moved away and we lost contact. As an adult, Frank has just one friend and they enjoy computer games.

Gradually, Frank became competent in practical self-help tasks; he could load the washing machine and tumble drier, work the remote on the TV and set up the computer. He continued to be oblivious to pain. His head is covered in small scars where he ran into doors, fell off his bike or fell over his own feet. I remember that awful feeling when his social worker came to visit and would comment on the number of hospital visits we had made.

Photographs show Frank on my husband's shoulders, or snuggled under my arm. He has blond hair and blue eyes, very pale skin and although his lips are puckered to kiss me, I remember I had to prompt him to do this. He now kisses me goodbye on a Monday morning, but is unable to do the reassuring pat on the back or the wave goodbye that I see other sons do to their aging mothers.

Other photos show us having fun and I'm pleased that when we look at them, Frank remembers these good times – buried in cold snow when we fell into a pit and laughing as we sledged down a hill on tea trays; feeding our sandwiches to the sheep, and siting in the garden in the freezing cold with our hoods up. A unique little family thinking this was normal.

Every now and then we would venture to invite a friend from school, but they only ever came once. Rough and tumble play would get out of control and Frank would strangle or punch them when he became over excited. We would try to play cards, but he didn't get turn taking, and we realised we were spending more time with the visiting child. LEGO®, colouring, and jigsaws worked well and reading started to become an obsession.

The psychotherapy sessions extended and continued for five years and Frank seemed calmer. To the list of activities we added judo – too rough; horse-riding – didn't like it; swimming club – made his deafness worse; but Frank said he was content to play at home or play in the field with the gang of boys. He was always on the edge of the field, and only in the football team when my husband went out to play. He would spend a long time running up and down before the ball was passed his way.

At 11 years of age, Frank returned to mainstream school. He was in a class with a teacher who had special needs experience. The system in our county provided middle school education with transfer to secondary school at 13. Sadly, this was a difficult period where our rhythm and patterns started to unwind and our relationship with Frank became very confrontational.

Frank found it difficult to be in a group of 30 children after the small specialist setting. In the small EBD unit, his teacher was interested in the way he liked to learn. He wasn't a child who could listen, so there were lots of drawings with simple explanations. Rehearsal for outings with exciting things to see and touch made sense of his confusing world. Frank still remembers his favourite visit to Bird World. We would get a home–school diary, so we were in touch with his moods and anxieties, and an occasional phone call to explain when there had been a meltdown.

Now, we could see two types of behaviour emerging on a daily basis: absolute rage when things weren't going his way, and meltdown when things didn't make sense. Frank spent more time in his bedroom watching TV, playing on the computer and, to be honest, we were both relieved.

I had been promoted to a deputy-head post and my husband was working in construction, so we were both tired. At Frank's case review, this new behaviour was put down to adolescence and this made sense. Sadly, we stopped enjoying his company, became irritated at his non-compliance and infuriated by his stupid rituals. However, the bond to care for him was still incredibly strong and I felt a powerful maternal drive.

Once again, my husband gave up work and started walking Frank to school every day. He would meet with the teacher and share concerns that something wasn't right. We then saw a new educational psychologist and social worker and a received a new diagnosis – social phobia with high anxiety! We were a nuclear family, with no previous experience of children and we had created a secure but restricted world for Frank. Well, of course that made sense, but it didn't give us the practical help that we craved. I don't think we felt blame, just frustration.

A referral was made to St George's Hospital for family therapy, with a caution that there would be a long waiting list. We followed the positive suggestions that we took Frank to a youth club and a football club. We took Frank for several sessions and then tried to follow other parents by leaving him at the door. Of course, he never went in; he would hide until it was time for us to pick him up and then emerge with the others. It was only when he broke down and cried that this emerged and of course we cried too, because we couldn't make it right.

School was starting to go wrong. His kindly teacher said he was being bullied, but the headteacher said he was the bully. His head was put down the toilet – yes, she said, but only because he swore at the other children. His bag went missing – yes, she said, but only because he was careless. Two events led to a confrontation. The headteacher phoned me at work to say Frank had flooded the toilets. Oh, the joy of being able to tell her he was at home with mumps! Then he had carved his name in a wall with a Stanley knife. He might have done this, but on the day in question he was safely in his therapy session. The alleged danger that Frank posed to others quickly led to a recommendation for residential education. The psychologist was worried that if Frank failed at secondary school he would be excluded and then out of the system for a long time.

We viewed three specialist schools for 'maladjusted boys', frighteningly bleak, staffed by physical education teachers. Eventually, we looked at a private residential school and this was just right. Small, individual areas, a key worker system, and weekly phone calls home. Frank progressed academically and made a few friends. The knowledgeable headteacher suggested Asperger's, as he felt that many of the pupils once described as EBD fitted this diagnosis. I disagreed, as I thought I knew what autism was, but I had only worked with children at the more severe end of what was described as the 'autism continuum'. Structure and strategies started to work at school and Frank looked calmer, but he became more solitary when he came home.

At last, the referral to St George's Hospital came to fruition. We went as a family, but the clinical psychologist decided she would work with us first. Slowly, the behaviour patterns started to make sense. We were allowed to grieve for the little boy we dreamed of looking after and caring for. We were praised for our positive approach and consistency, and for not rejecting Frank. The lack of bonding was not blamed on our inadequate parenting. Frank, a young man with abilities but complex needs, emerged. Now we had a positive plan. We asked Frank if he would like to be adopted by us, but he said this didn't make any sense, so we continued as his foster parents.

The work with the clinical psychologist gave us permission to start rebuilding our own social lives. While Frank was at school, we went skiing. I started going abroad with a friend, my husband took up cycling. We could accept Frank as he was and reduce the pressures and demands. If he stayed in his bedroom, this was fine because we knew that a football match would draw him out. Going out for an Indian meal was stressful, but a takeaway was fine. Frank liked to cycle into town alone, when he could follow his preferred route. We had several years after leaving school when he succeeded at the local college, gained a few qualifications and worked in a kitchen at the weekend. He had driving lessons but after failing the test once, never wanted to repeat the experience again. I gave Frank driving lessons for his 40th birthday and although the instructor reported that he was a steady and safe driver, the thought of the test overwhelmed him and there were lots of sleepless nights.

The next part of my story, when Frank was aged 18–30 is painful, and sadly reflects the dilemma faced by many young people with special needs coming out of care, even today. Yet another new young social worker appeared on the scene. She took Frank out and started the transition plan for him to leave us at 18. We resisted, saying that Frank was vulnerable and naive, but Frank was enticed by the thought of his own flat, and a leaving care grant of £300.

The flat turned out to be a room in a shared house. It was dirty and smelly, and we didn't recognise the smell of cannabis. We helped Frank paint the room and foster grandparents provided practical house-warming gifts – his own kettle, a mini fridge, a TV and bright china. Frank told us that he had got a place to do a course in tourism at college and his social worker said she would handle the supervision.

We tried to let go and leave Frank to transition to his new life. We phoned once a week and visited every two or three weeks. I sent cards and his foster grandma popped in when she was shopping. She first alerted us to the deterioration in Frank's personal hygiene. We made a drop-by visit and found that his room was nearly bare. Apparently, he had 'lent' his possessions to new friends that he had met in a nightclub! Frank was unable to tell us anything about his course, so my husband phoned the college. But unfortunately, it seemed it would be a breach of confidentiality to tell us anything. For goodness sake, this young man had special needs.

At 20, Frank was not at college or at work and was managing on benefits, but this was not our problem anymore. We continued to phone, but this became monthly until we had a call from him to say his girlfriend had just had a baby. I blamed my husband, as he did the sex education, I blamed the social worker, but when I phoned social services to ask for some support for this new family, I discovered to my horror that Frank was no longer receiving supervision because he had said he didn't want it.

My husband was resigned and able to take a step back and not get involved, although he later said this was a traumatic period for him, and he wondered how he had failed this little boy. I rallied Grandma, and we arranged to visit them. Frank lived in his room in the supported living house, and she lived on the floor below with her three little girls and the new baby boy. They shared similar stories, both in care, both attending special school and both leaving home at 18.

Frank picked up the baby but didn't make eye contact or any baby sounds, and lost interest when the baby cried, putting him down to turn on the TV. I recognised the significance of his difficulties and felt sadness, knowing that this relationship would not last.

When we heard from Frank again, it was a desperate phone call. He had been sleeping rough and he hadn't got anywhere to live. We drove to pick him up in a park. He was a mess but didn't want to stay with us. We fed him, bought new clothes from the charity shop and rang social services. We got sympathetic advice and were told that he needed to find accommodation in a hostel to get on the housing list. As you can't book a bed, we drove him to the hostel. You can only stay three nights, so we arranged for Grandma to pick him up and drive him to the next hostel ten miles away. This pattern went on for several weeks. Frank then told us a friend had offered him a bed in a shared house but he wouldn't say where. Frank then became a cannabis user and we knew we could not help anymore.

Grandma took over – and we admired her determination. She called the housing office and found out how to get him on the housing list. She went to the social service office with all his early paperwork and demanded help. She took Frank to her doctor, who referred him to a psychiatrist, but in the meantime, he had a psychiatric breakdown and was sectioned. His new diagnosis was paranoid schizophrenia. A clinical psychologist reminded us of the 'long-playing record' strategy. We phoned social services every day, and we wrote letters, or rather sent the same one with second, third, fourth request written on the top to the housing department, and one day we were told that Frank was going to be given a flat. It was on the 22nd floor of a tower block, but Frank agreed.

Frank's mental health deteriorated again and this time he went to the police and asked for help. They did help because he was sectioned again, but I think his current phobia about the police relates to this incident.

For several years, Frank was under the care of a psychiatric team and this allowed him to return home, but last year government cuts meant this support was removed. So, all that happens now is that he attends the local hospital once a month to have his blood cells checked.

Last week, Frank had his Disability Living Allowance refused and he failed to score any points to get a Personal Independent Payment. This weekend I will spend time reassuring him that we can get this sorted. I will write on his behalf, explaining how difficult it is for him to cope daily and the fact that he is coping is due to the support he receives from me. I will watch for the tell-tale signs – more panic attacks, sweat dripping down his face, phone calls where he is incoherent, his thoughts and speech racing – and try to think of something nice to distract him. Currently it's bacon sandwiches for breakfast and I won't moan that he likes eight rashers between two slices of bread. That's a whole packet!

The iceberg model is a great way of understanding Frank's autism and mental health. What you see can be explained, but under the surface, so much is confusing. The government programmes of action are so positive about the possible help he should receive, but it's difficult to access this. I feel sad for the life he might have led as an adult with a little more appropriate help.

But I'm certainly not a refrigerated foster mum – I'm not giving up.

Chapter 15

THANDO AND TIISETSO

(SOUTH AFRICA)

Having tried to conceive for 19 years, it felt like a dream when I was told I was pregnant! Dutifully, I attended all antenatal clinic visits to the last day. It was indeed a challenging pregnancy; with high blood pressure, swollen feet and terrible skin, I looked like a baby elephant facing the other way, and I wanted to scrub off the darker patches that I was developing. I thought I was going to give birth to a very dark-skinned baby, notwithstanding the fact that he was going to be overdue by four weeks!

When I went for the last scan, where the doctor wanted to verify the sex, the baby was too huge to fit on the scan and I was only on my 45th week! The doctor immediately prescribed tablets to induce labour, but these did not work. I was given three doses of these tablets and still nothing. I think on the third day the pain started and lasted for a good 15 hours. Eventually, I gave birth at 9.30pm on 3 March 1994.

When Tiisetso (weighing 3.5kg) was born, he didn't cry, and even when the doctor gave him a gentle clap on the buttocks, the crying was so lazy it was as if he had just woken up. Straight after birth,

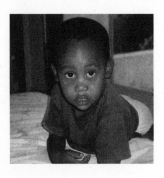

he was put in the incubator for three days as he had jaundice and they wanted to monitor him.

Once at home, boy, did I have a hungry baby, who never stopped sucking. I had to be treated for cracked nipples from the way he was sucking, and he did not stop.

Months went by, years went by, until he reached the year of going to a nursery. I was a very busy person and I didn't notice that Tiisetso had missed some milestones; he only started walking at 15 months, and there was nothing verbal, not even 'mama'. I missed these warning signs.

At the time, I was working for Young & Rubicam as an account manager, looking after the biggest account they had. Then in May 1996, I moved to the Office of The President (Nelson Mandela). When I worked for Young & Rubicam, Tiisetso attended a nursery school near the office. I got complaints that he did not understand instructions, nor academic deliberations in the class environment. After about six months they told me not to bring him back. This is when my frustrations began. I was so frustrated as my career was beginning to flourish, I was extremely busy, and did not have the time to think about, let alone address, these reported problems.

Tiisetso went to several nursery schools and crèches. At the time, autism was hardly known in South Africa and in between successful school placements, believe it or not, I had to take him with me to work at the Union Buildings (the official seat of the

South African government)! I explained everything to Nelson Mandela and he did not have a problem at all, and said that I should let him know if I need financial support. I told him I did not know what assistance I needed.

One day in 1997, I met with a doctor, and she was kind and told me that my child had the characteristics of autism and I should take him for an assessment to a paediatrician called Dr Joan Wagner. Dr Wagner assessed him and wrote a report with a diagnosis of pervasive developmental disorder, which impacts on communication and social interaction.

I applied to the Autism Unit at the Johannesburg Hospital School Unit for Autism but there was no space at the time. I took Tiisetso to The Key School, which was private and therefore expensive, but I did this as I waited for a place at the Autism Unit at the Hospital School.

At the time of the diagnosis I started experiencing rejection from family members and the community at large. Tiisetso would scream and have tantrums, lying flat on the floor not wanting to go anywhere. I had to buy a dog's harness to put around his chest so that we could go out, but this did not work because as soon as I put it on him, he would lie on the floor and not move.

Tiisetso was still in diapers and I was still breastfeeding him when he was 4 years old. My daughter felt that I should take him off the breast, so that I could go to work, or visit friends, as she knew I also needed time to myself. It became a struggle to take him off the breast. At this time, I had to buy a pram as he was so heavy to carry or move. Several times he fell out of the pram, but he never cried when this happened.

The challenges continued and I felt isolated as family members would arrange parties that I was invited to as long as I didn't bring my 'mad' child with me. I would respond by thanking them for the invitation, but declining as I would not leave my child, nor lock him in the back room. Trips with Tiisetso to shopping malls would result in people staring at us, or saying I had a spoilt child.

I did try employing nannies – probably up to about 20 nannies – but most thought Tiisetso was a disrespectful child and they used to hit him.

After two years at The Key School I saw no progress. He also attended MaylilI Nursery School, but it only had a few classes for special needs. Eventually, the Autism Unit at the Johannesburg Hospital School called me to say there was space and he was accepted and screened for a particular class. It was then that I started seeing progress in Tiisetso and he grew to be this precious child who is now very capable and able to do things for himself.

Tiisetso has two siblings: a sister and a brother. He communicates with both of them, especially his brother, as he identifies with him since they are the only men in this household. He would get upset when his brother disappeared, and we did not see him for several months. The day his brother resurfaced, Tiisetso's excitement was brilliant to see. He loves his sister too, but he never sees her as she stays in Sandton. Time and again he would imitate his brother's township lingo.

Tiisetso is basically a healthy eater. I did not understand this until I started observing his behaviour when eating. First, he will not eat with his plate on his lap. He will only eat when his food is on a set table. Thanks to the Johannesburg Hospital School, he has good table manners. His favourites are fruit, fish and, sometimes, red meat but not that often. He has a big appetite. He makes sure he has his Kellogg's cereal in the morning. At midday, I must be ready with lunch, and in between meals, he has fruit. There is more fruit in my house than anything else! He does not like cakes or creamy stuff. He is basically very healthy. The only problem is that his gums bleed during his sleep and he has a crowding of teeth, which I think causes the bleeding.

Tiisetso grew to be an outstanding teenager. There is one thing that I have to mention and that is when he started growing pubic hair, he used to pull the hair out, sometimes making himself bleed but, like many children with autism, he did not feel pain, and the plucking of the hair did not bother him. This stage upset me a lot as I did not know how to get him to understand that this hair growth was natural. One good day when he was in the bathroom and he started pulling, I stopped him and showed him that I also have pubic hair and after that, he never did it again, but just stared at his pubic hair and put soap all over it and washed it.

At school, he was such an organised boy, and he worked in the kitchen – he really hates dirt. They would wash dishes and cutlery, then pack them in the cupboard, and if they were not packed in an orderly fashion, he would unpack them and start washing them again. He felt unless they were packed properly they could not be clean! He would sweep under people's feet if he was not satisfied that the floor had been properly cleaned!

Tiisetso was doing so well that he used to work on a computer. He is able to read some text and he loves gardening. I bought a whole lot of spinach that he planted for me. He was also taught to bake, and prepare sandwiches in the tuckshop. His other interest is watches; we can be walking in a mall and he will stop at a jewellery shop and keep saying 'watch'. I once bought him a watch from American Swiss, but now I buy from cheap Chinese shops and he has almost 50 watches that he changes every day.

Tiisetso had a phase of walking around naked in the house even when there were people around! I had to intervene to tell him he could not do that when there were family or friends visiting. I have also had to teach him to close the toilet door when he is using it. I requested that the school make signs saying 'No entry'. Additionally, when he is in the toilet, he strips off his clothes and packs them behind the bucket until he finishes what he is doing in the toilet, then he dresses.

Tiisetso hated my grandchild with passion. Nkululeko would try and play with him and he would punch him. To prevent this, I started a social story programme, which lasted for about five weeks.

After that he stopped hitting him. In the car, he takes the passenger seat in front and no one else is allowed to sit there! He loves music dearly; he can listen to something once and then he can sing the song word for word. He likes Luther Vandross, Joe, and the O'Jays. And he sings with their voice.

Tiisetso started working at the sheltered workshop early this year, doing different things, but they discovered his interest in manufacturing fly swatters. He was manufacturing one fly swatter within a minute. He started working at 8.30am and by 3pm he had about three boxes of complete fly swatters. I discovered that he was bullied by the elderly guys who just sat and watched him work; they would sleep, as they knew he would not report them. Something bad must have happened there as now he does not want to go back.

I recently discovered that he is scared of heights, dogs and cats. Strangely enough, as he was growing up, we used to have a Rottweiler which he used to sleep and play with. I am not sure what happened in the interim. He also loves to clean the house and he does it with pride and is very organised. Tiisetso is obsessed with photographs; he will look at them for hours and you must not try to take them away because there will be war.

I am so proud of my son, who, through many adversities, has come an exceptionally long way.